GLORIA IN EXCELSIS DEO

GLORY TO GOD IN THE HIGHEST

A Christmas Work for Choir, Soloists, and Instruments

Created and Arranged by
TOM FETTKE

Orchestrations by Bruce Greer

The creator of Gloria in Excelsis Deo wishes to thank
Bill and Robin Wolaver, Ken Bible, and Bruce Greer
for their significant creative contributions to this Christmas work.

Copyright © 1998 by Pilot Point Music.   All rights reserved.   Litho in U.S.A.

Kansas City, MO 64141

CONTENTS

PART I — GOOD TIDINGS OF GREAT JOY ... 3
OVERTURE AND OPENING
Includes:
- Angels We Have Heard on High
- Carol of the Bells
- Thou That Tellest Good Tidings

PART II — GOD IS WITH US ... 17
Includes:
- Behold, a Virgin Shall Conceive
- God Is with Us! Alleluia!
- "Alleluias" from CHRISTMAS ORATORIO

PART III — FOR UNTO US A CHILD IS BORN ... 25
Includes:
- Jesus
- For unto Us a Child Is Born

PART IV — THE NATIVITY ... 35
Includes:
- Silent Night! Holy Night!
- Lullaby for a King
- Love Has Come!

PART V — GLORY TO GOD IN THE HIGHEST ... 48
Includes:
- And Suddenly
- Glory to God in the Highest

PART VI — JESUS, SHEPHERDS, AND CHILDREN ... 58
Includes:
- While Shepherds Watched Their Flocks
- Christmas Is a Time for Children
- Hark! the Herald Angels Sing
- Go, Tell It on the Mountain

PART VII — REJOICE WITH EXCEEDING GREAT JOY ... 68
Includes:
- Nations Will Come to Your Light
- Concerto in G Minor
- Rejoice with Exceeding Great Joy

PART VIII — GLORY TO THE LAMB OF CHRISTMAS ... 77
Includes:
- The Lamb of Christmas
- The Lamb Appears

PART IX — GLORIA! ... 88
Includes:
- Gloria Fanfare
- The Glory of the Lord
- And the Glory of the Lord
- Light Is Shining All Around
- Hallelujah Chorus

Clip Art ... 116

Part I
GOOD TIDINGS OF GREAT JOY
Overture and Opening
includes
Angels We Have Heard on High
Carol of the Bells
O Thou that Tellest Good Tidings

*Arranged by Tom Fettke
and Bruce Greer*

*Music, Traditional French Melody. Arr. © 1998 by Pilot Point Music (ASCAP). All rights reserved. Administered by The Copyright Company, 40 Music Square East, Nashville, TN 37203.

**Optional organ or additional keyboard instrument

*"Carol of the Bells"

*Music, Ukrainian Carol. Arr. © 1998 by Pilot Point Music (ASCAP). All rights reserved. Administered by The Copyright Company, 40 Music Square East, Nashville, TN 37203.

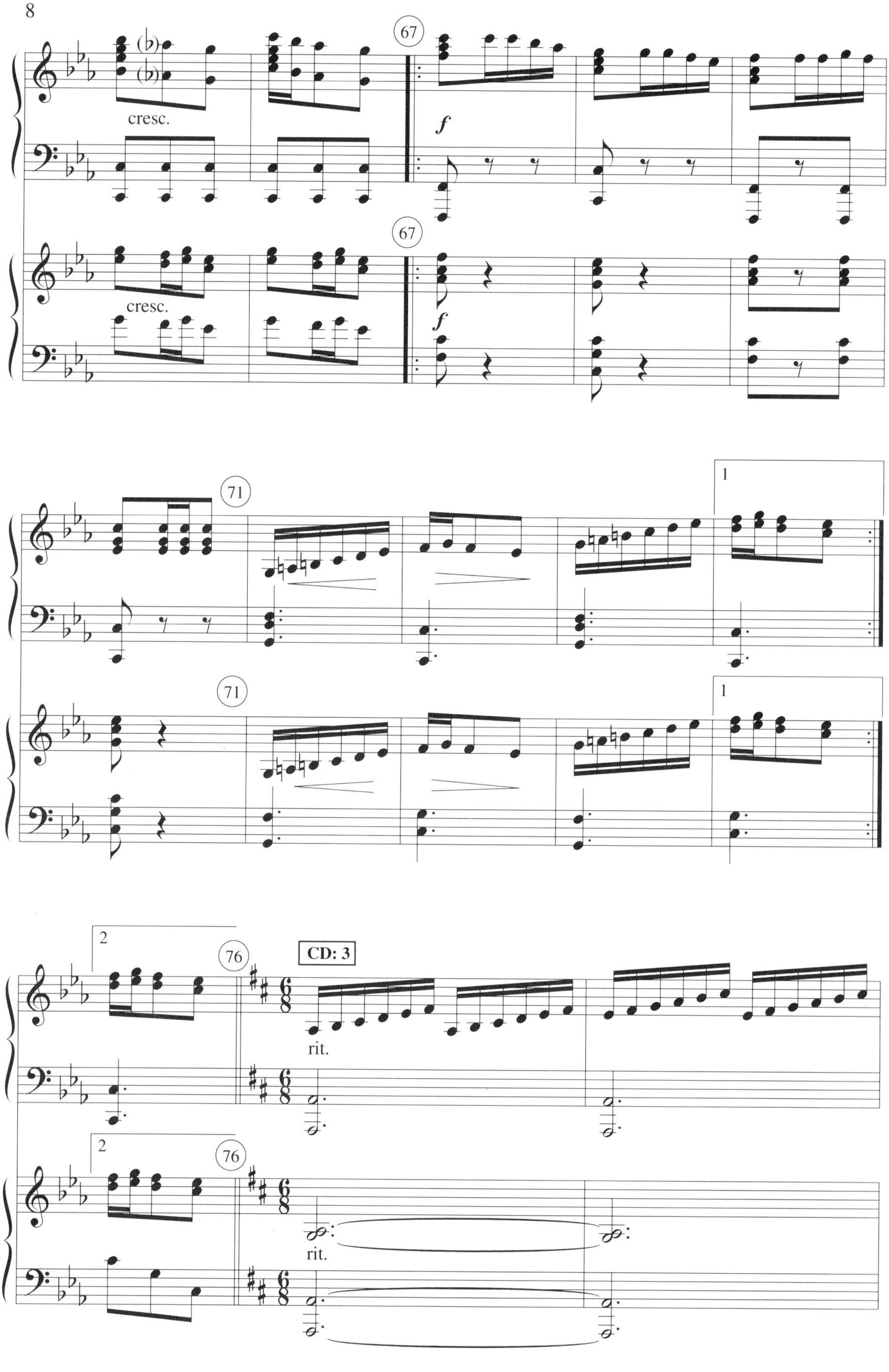
67
cresc.
f
71
1
2
76
CD: 3
rit.

*Words adapted from Scripture; Music by George Frederick Handel. Arr. © 1998 by Pilot Point Music (ASCAP). All rights reserved. Administered by The Copyright Company, 40 Music Square East, Nashville, TN 37203.

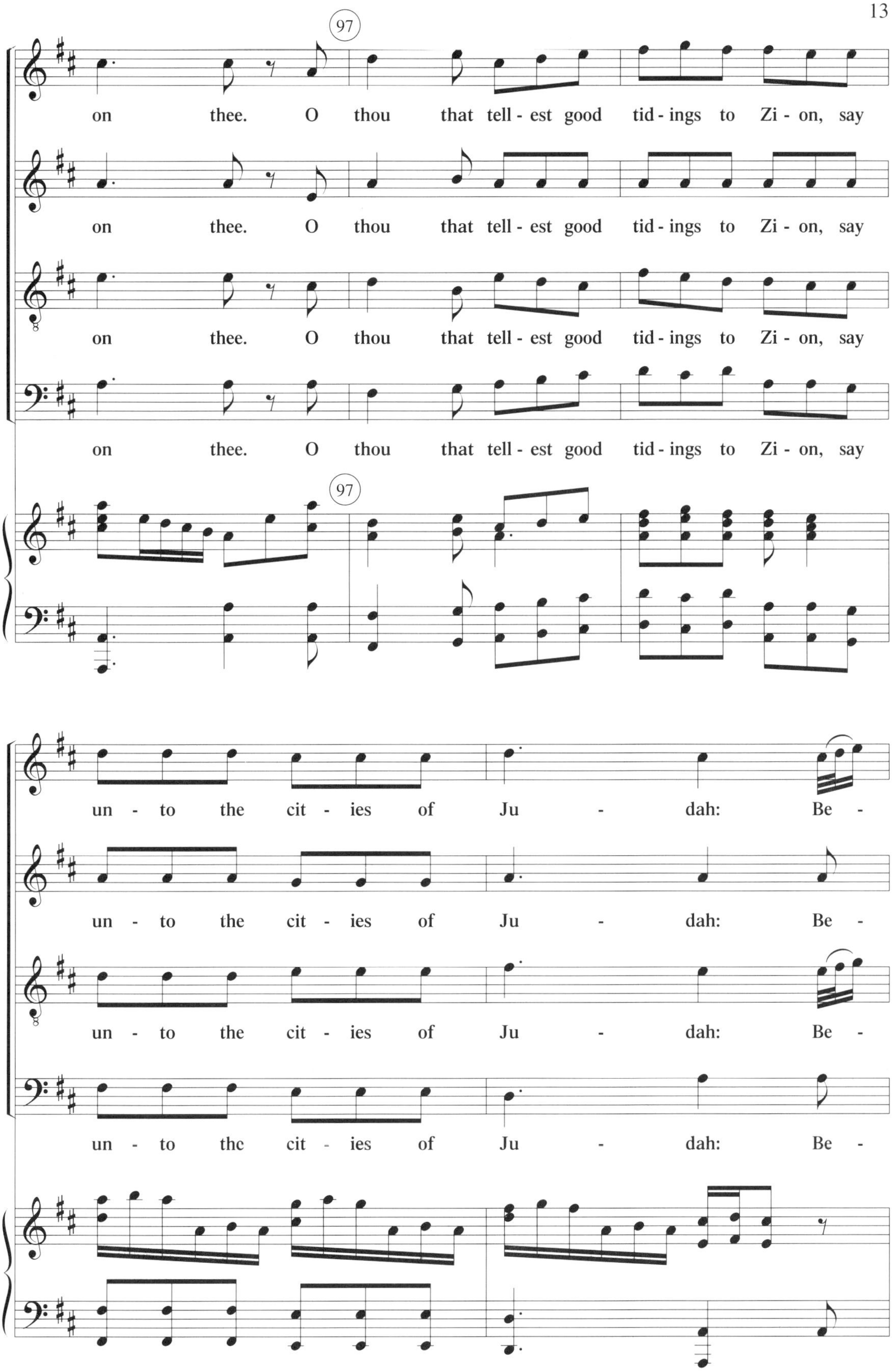
97
on thee. O thou that tell - est good tid - ings to Zi - on, say
on thee. O thou that tell - est good tid - ings to Zi - on, say
on thee. O thou that tell - est good tid - ings to Zi - on, say
on thee. O thou that tell - est good tid - ings to Zi - on, say
97
un - to the cit - ies of Ju - dah: Be -
un - to the cit - ies of Ju - dah: Be -
un - to the cit - ies of Ju - dah: Be -
un - to thc cit - ies of Ju - dah: Be -

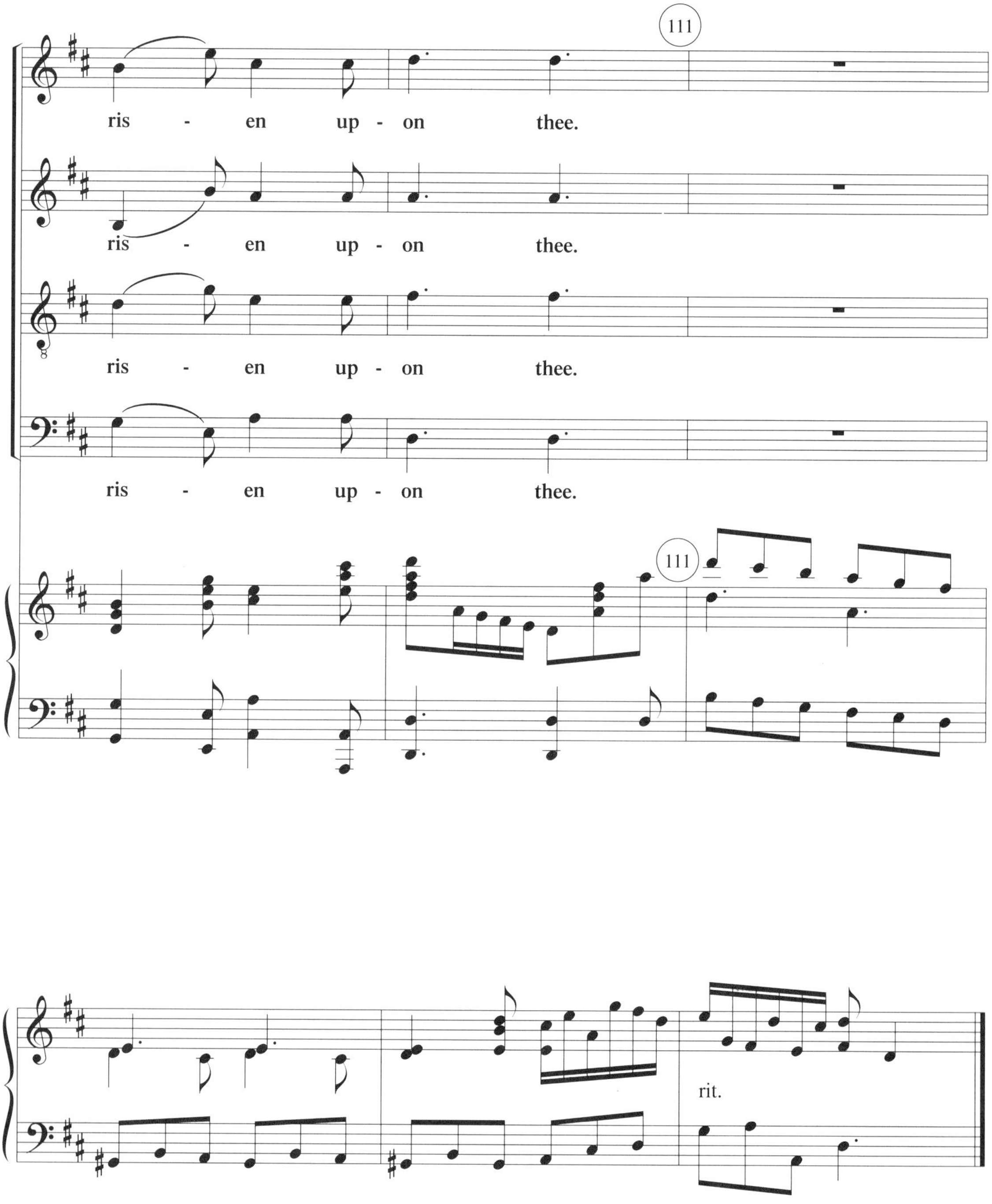
111
ris - en up - on thee.
ris - en up - on thee.
ris - en up - on thee.
ris - en up - on thee.
111
rit.

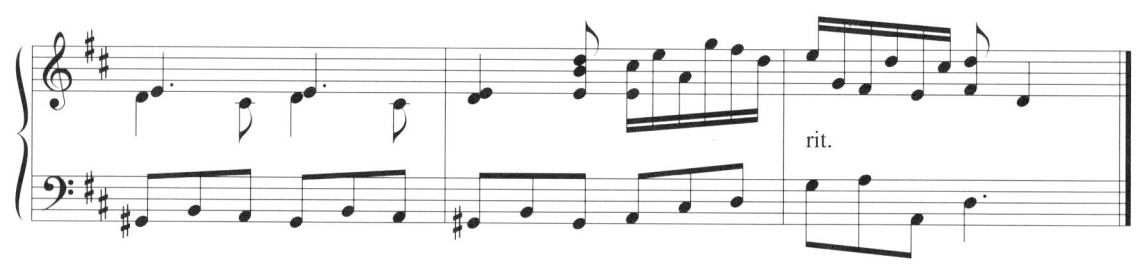

*Words adapted from Isaiah 7:14; Music by George Frederick Handel. Arr. © 1998 by Pilot Point Music (ASCAP). All rights reserved. Administered by The Copyright Company, 40 Music Square East, Nashville, TN 37203.

*Words by Ken Bible, Tom Fettke and Thomas Ken; Music from *Geistliche Kirchengesange*. Copyright © 1998 by Pilot Point Music (ASCAP). All rights reserved. Admin. by The Copyright Company, 40 Music Square E., Nashville, TN 37203.

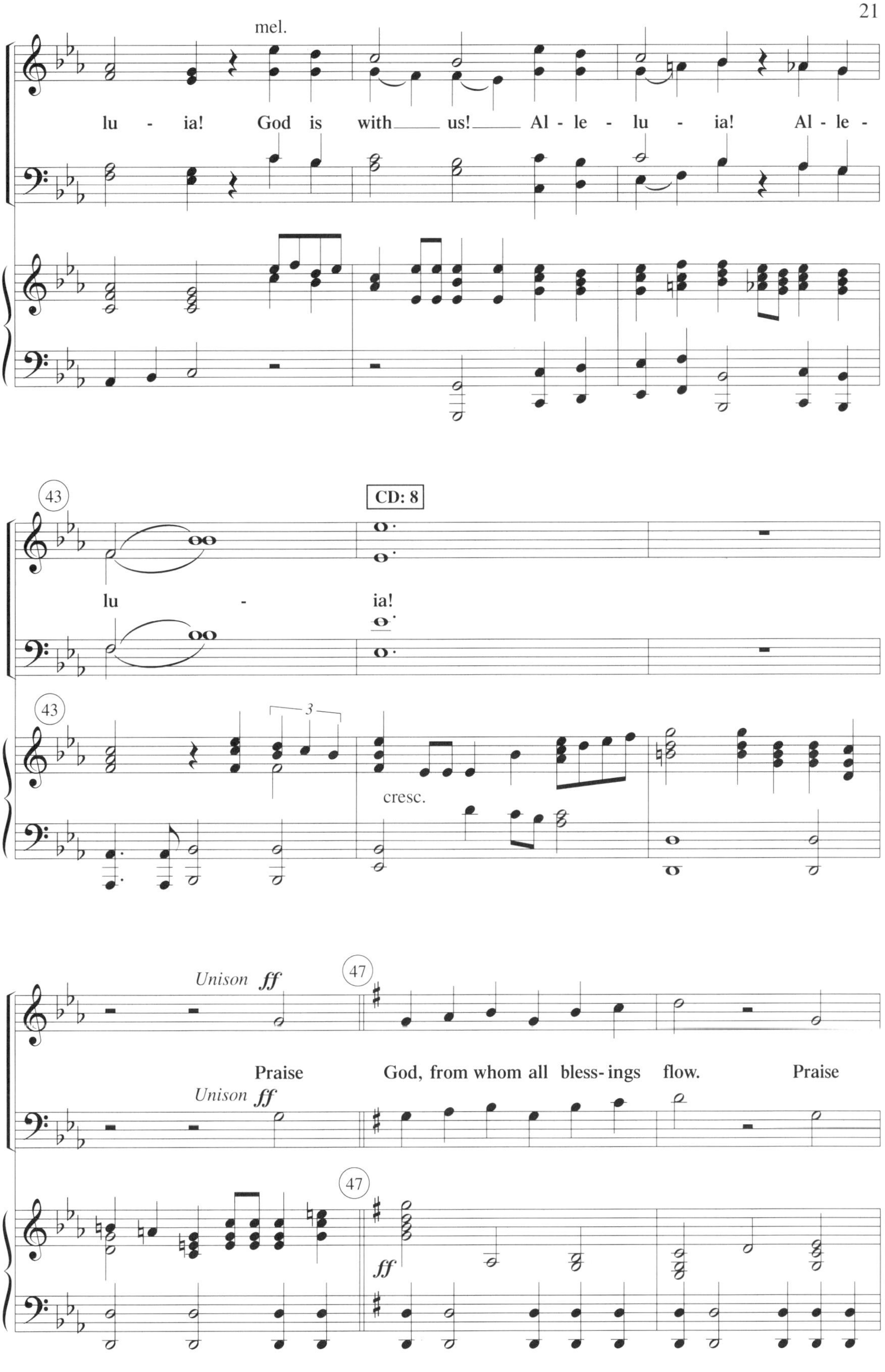
mel.
lu - ia! God is with us! Al - le - lu - ia! Al - le -
43
CD: 8
lu - ia!
3
cresc.
Unison ff
47
Praise God, from whom all bless-ings flow. Praise
ff

*"Alleluias from *Christmas Oratorio*"

*Words and Music by Camille Saint-Saens. Arr. © 1998 by Pilot Point Music (ASCAP). All rights reserved. Admin. by The Copyright Company, 40 Music Square East, Nashville, TN 37203.

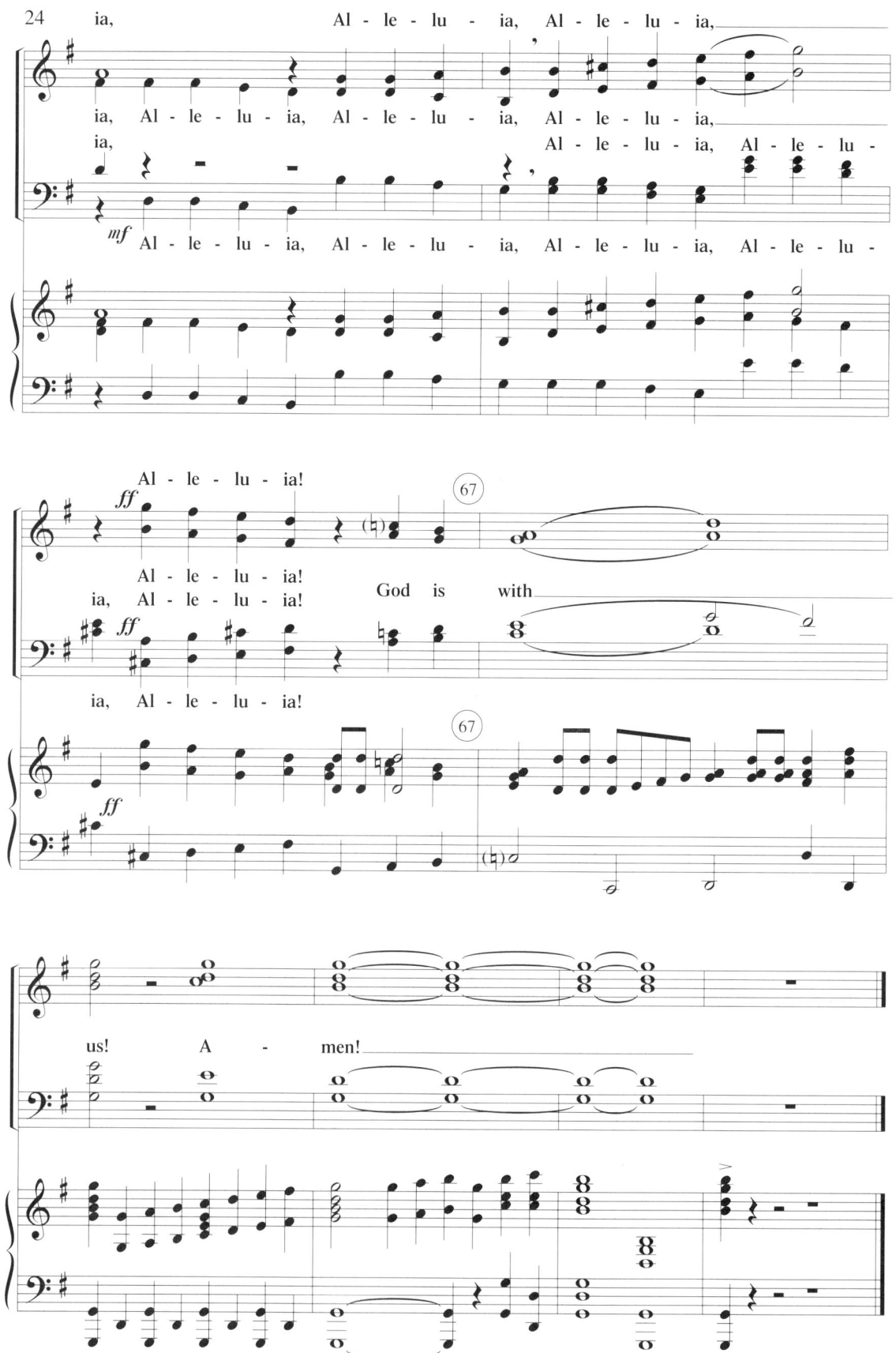

Part III
FOR UNTO US A CHILD IS BORN
includes
Jesus
For Unto Us a Child Is Born

Arranged by Tom Fettke

*Words by Ken Bible; Music by Johann Schop. Copyright © 1998 by Pilot Point Music (ASCAP). All rights reserved. Admin. by The Copyright Company, 40 Music Square E., Nashville, TN 37203.

*"For Unto Us a Child Is Born"

*Words adapted from Isaiah 9:6 by Robin Wolaver; Music by Bill Wolaver. Copyright © 1998 by Pilot Point Music (ASCAP). All rights reserved. Administered by The Copyright Company, 40 Music Square East, Nashville, TN 37203.

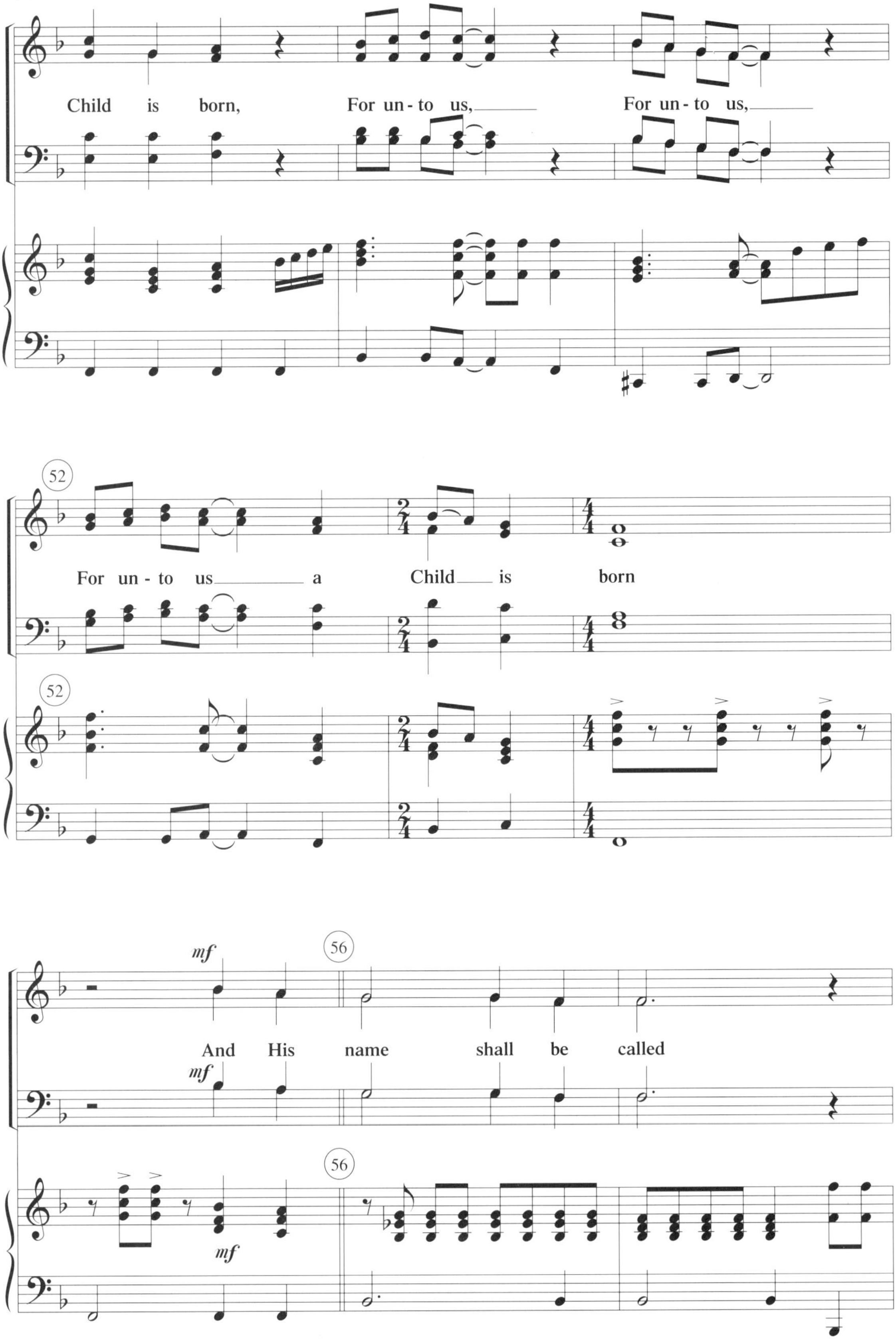
Child is born,
For un - to us,
For un - to us,
52
For un - to us a Child is born
52
mf
56
And His name shall be called
mf
56
mf

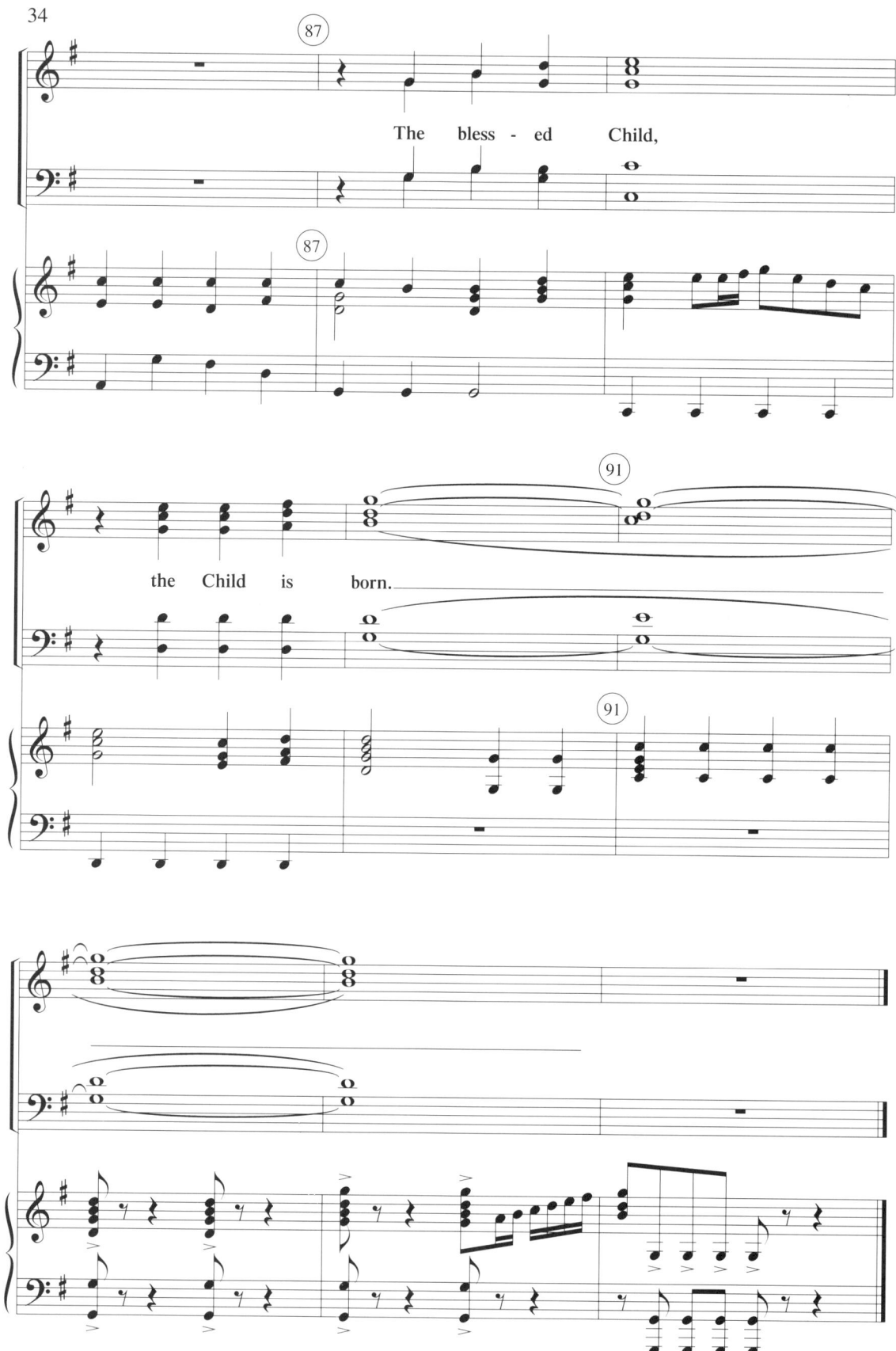

Part IV
THE NATIVITY
includes
Silent Night! Holy Night!
Lullaby for a King
Love Has Come!

Arranged by Tom Fettke

*Words by Joseph Mohr; Music by Franz Gruber. Arr. © 1998 by Pilot Point Music (ASCAP). All rights reserved. Admin. by The Copyright Company, 40 Music Square E., Nashville, TN 37203.

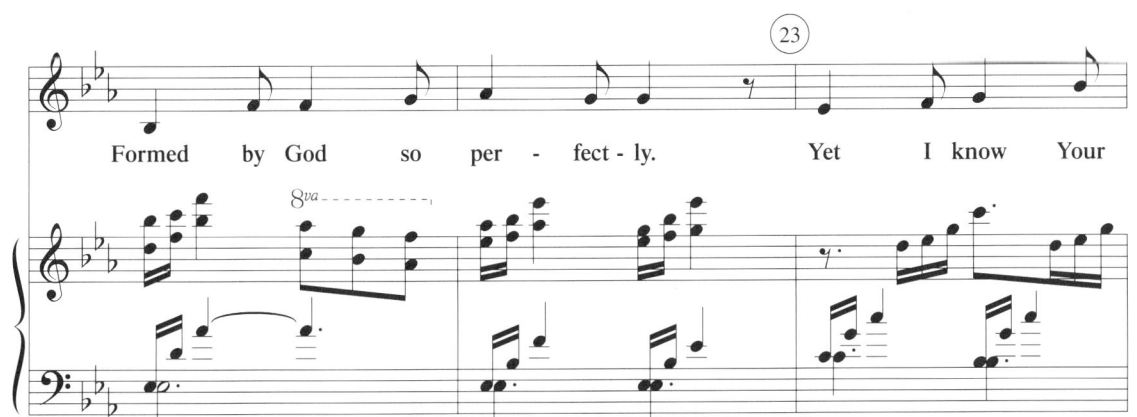

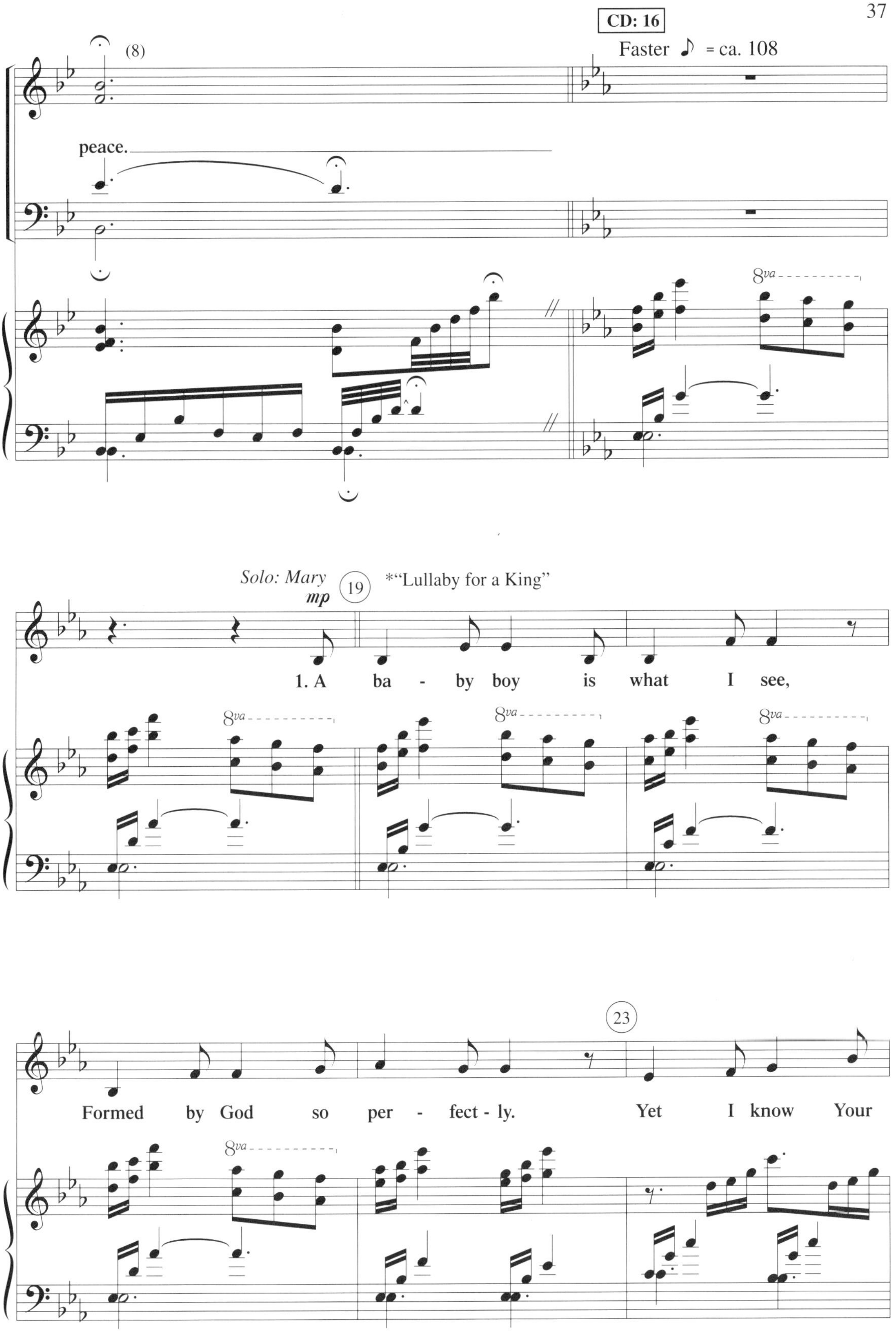
CD: 16
(8)
Faster ♪ = ca. 108
peace.
8va
Solo: Mary
mp
19
*"Lullaby for a King"
1. A ba - by boy is what I see,
8va
Formed by God so per - fect - ly.
23
Yet I know Your

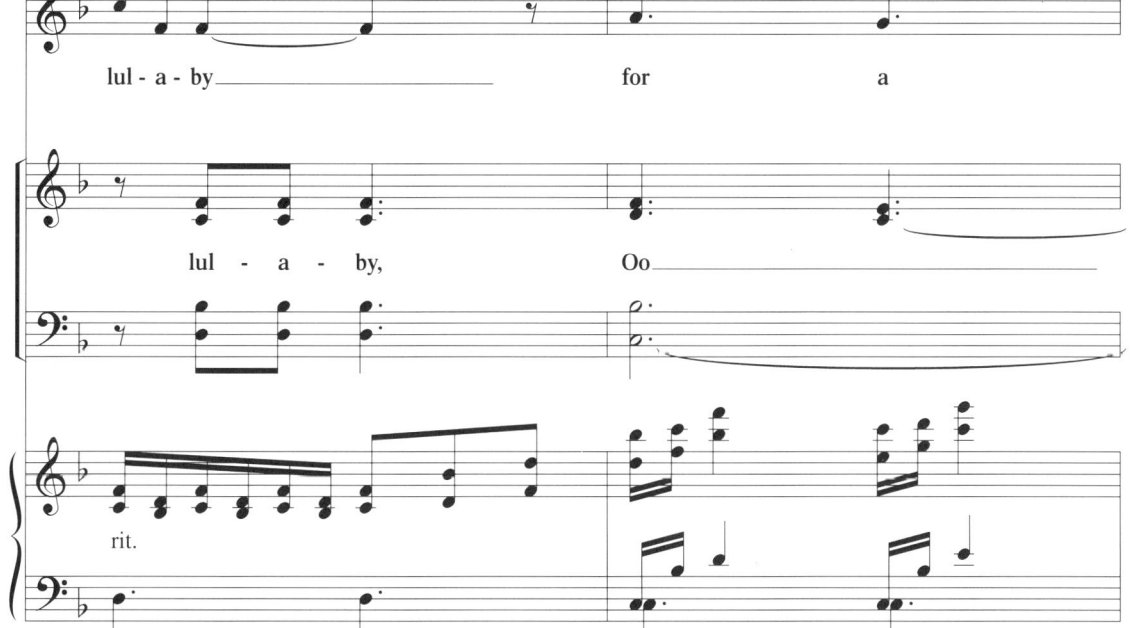

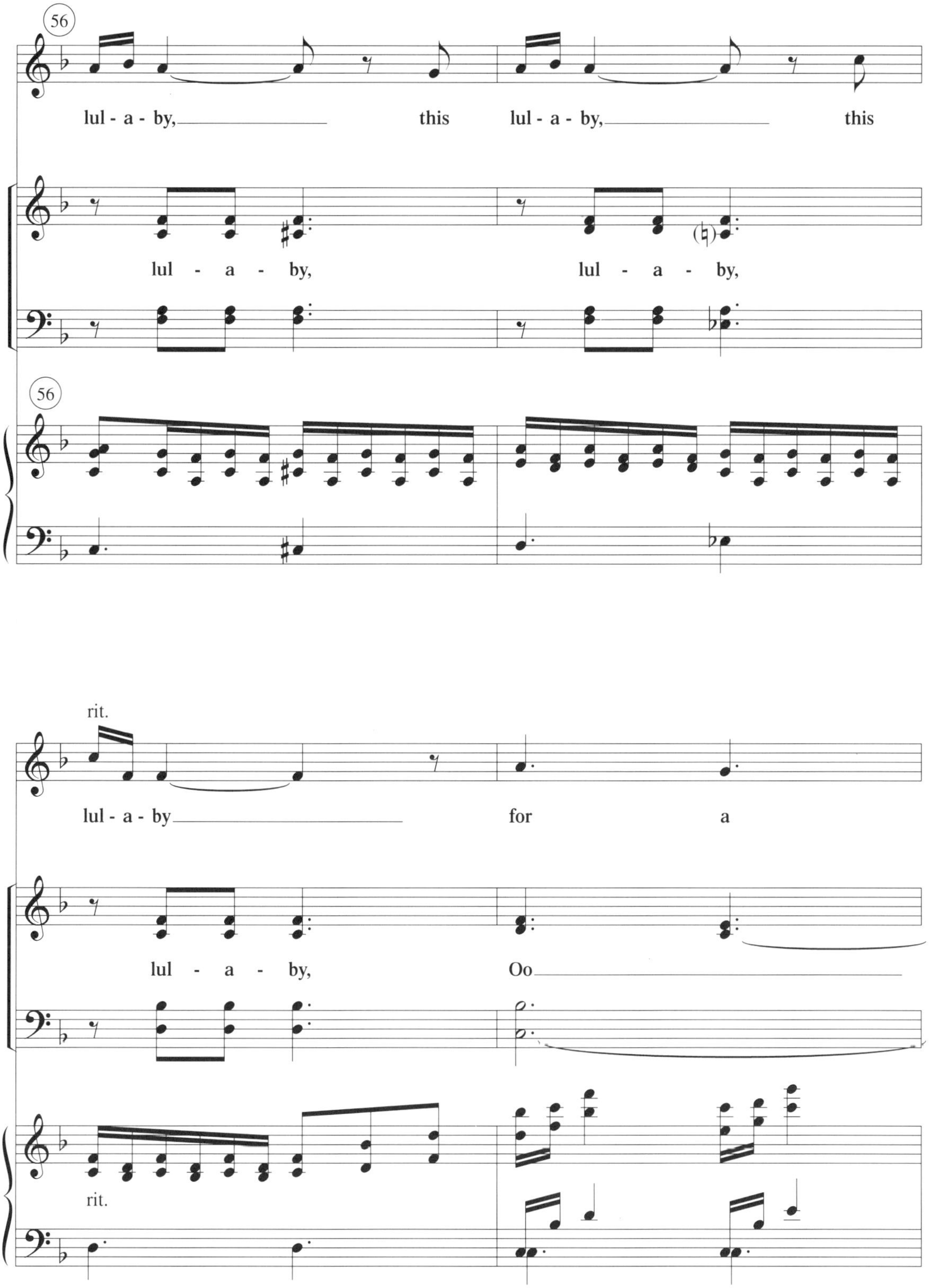
56
lul - a - by, this lul - a - by, this
lul - a - by, lul - a - by,
56
rit.
lul - a - by for a
lul - a - by, Oo
rit.

44

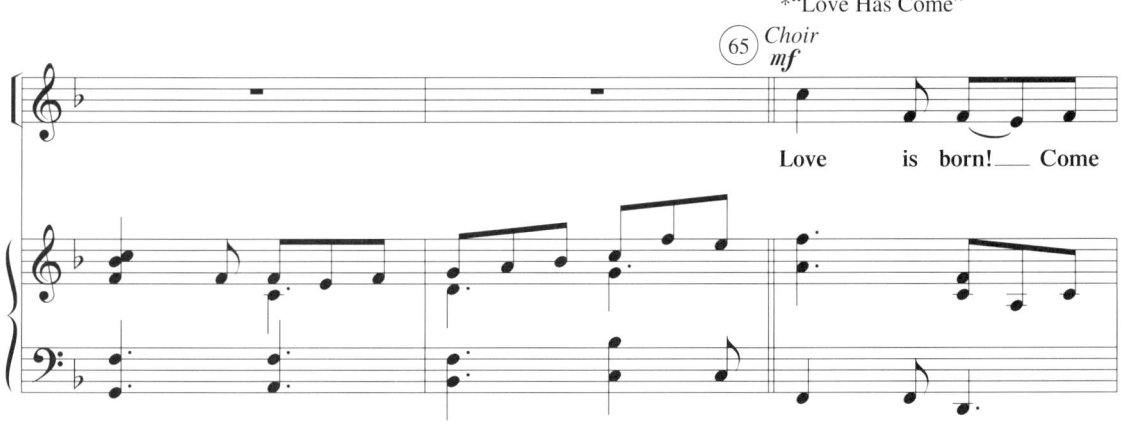

*Words by Ken Bible; Music, French Carol Melody. Copyright © 1996 Integrity's Hosanna! Music/ASCAP, c/o Integrity Music, Inc., Box 851622, Mobile, AL 36685-1622. All rights reserved. International copyright secured. Used by permission.

Part V
GLORY TO GOD IN THE HIGHEST
includes
And Suddenly
Glory to God in the Highest

*Arranged by Tom Fettke
and Bill Wolaver*

*Words adapted from Luke 2:13; Music by Camille Saint-Saens. Arr. © 1998 by Pilot Point Music (ASCAP). All rights reserved. Administered by The Copyright Company, 40 Music Square East., Nashville, TN 37203.

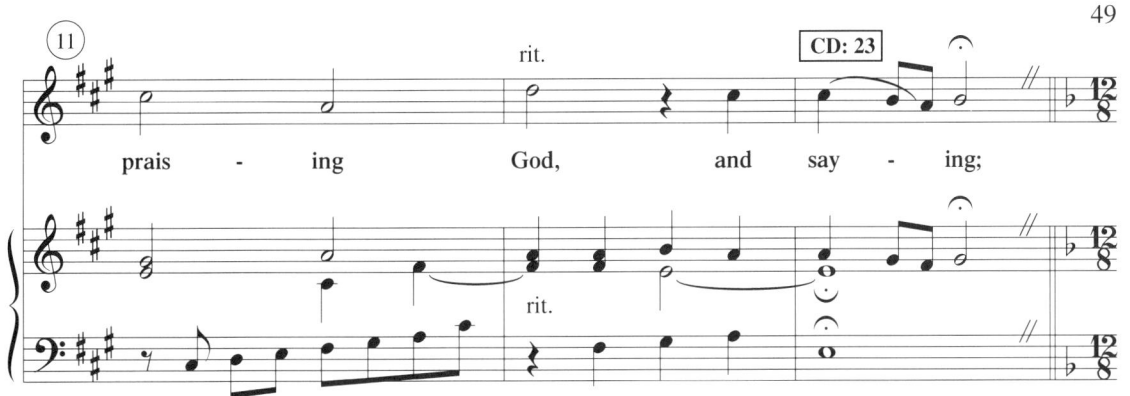

*"Glory to God in the Highest"

*Words adapted from Luke 2:14 by Robin Wolaver; Music by Bill Wolaver. Copyright © 1998 by Pilot Point Music (ASCAP). All rights reserved. Administered by The Copyright Company, 40 Music Square East, Nashville, TN 37203.

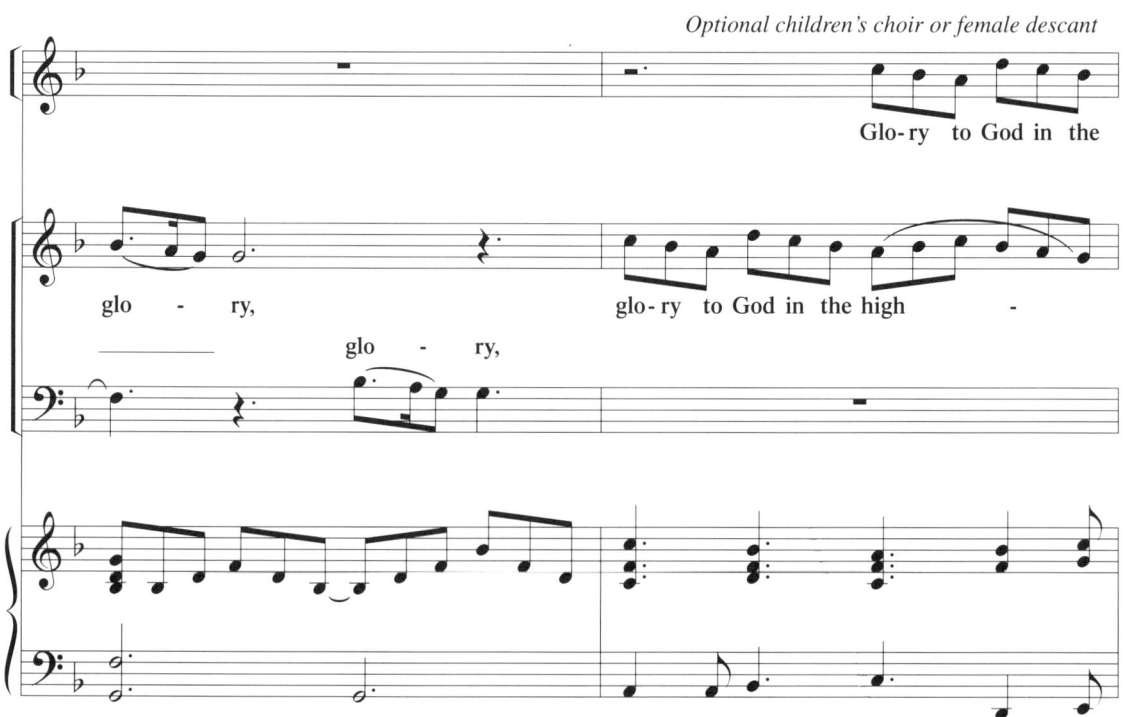

Optional children's choir or female descant

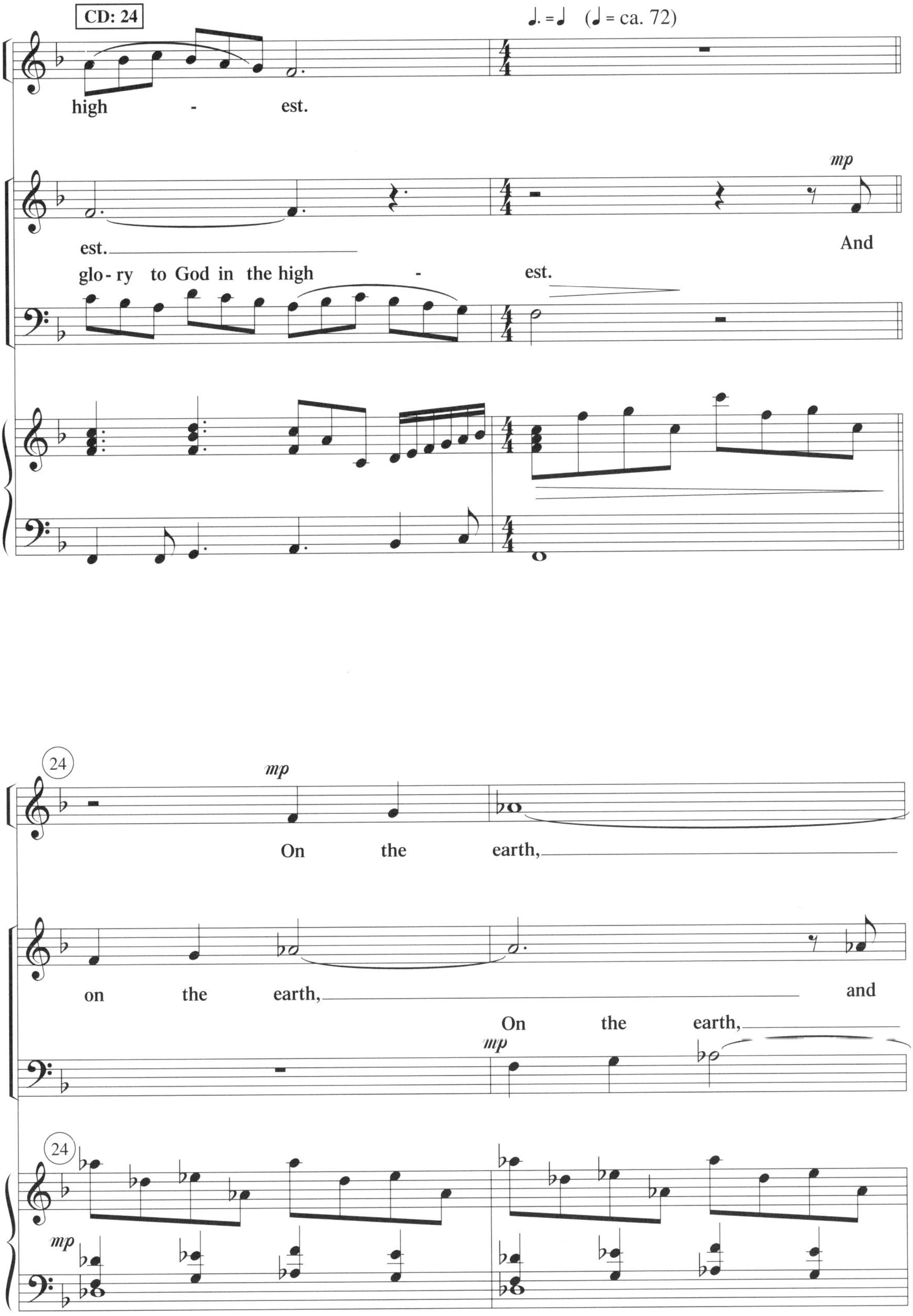
CD: 24
♩. = ♩ (♩ = ca. 72)
high - est.
mp
est.
And
glo - ry to God in the high - est.
24
mp
On the earth,
on the earth,
and
On the earth,
mp
24
mp

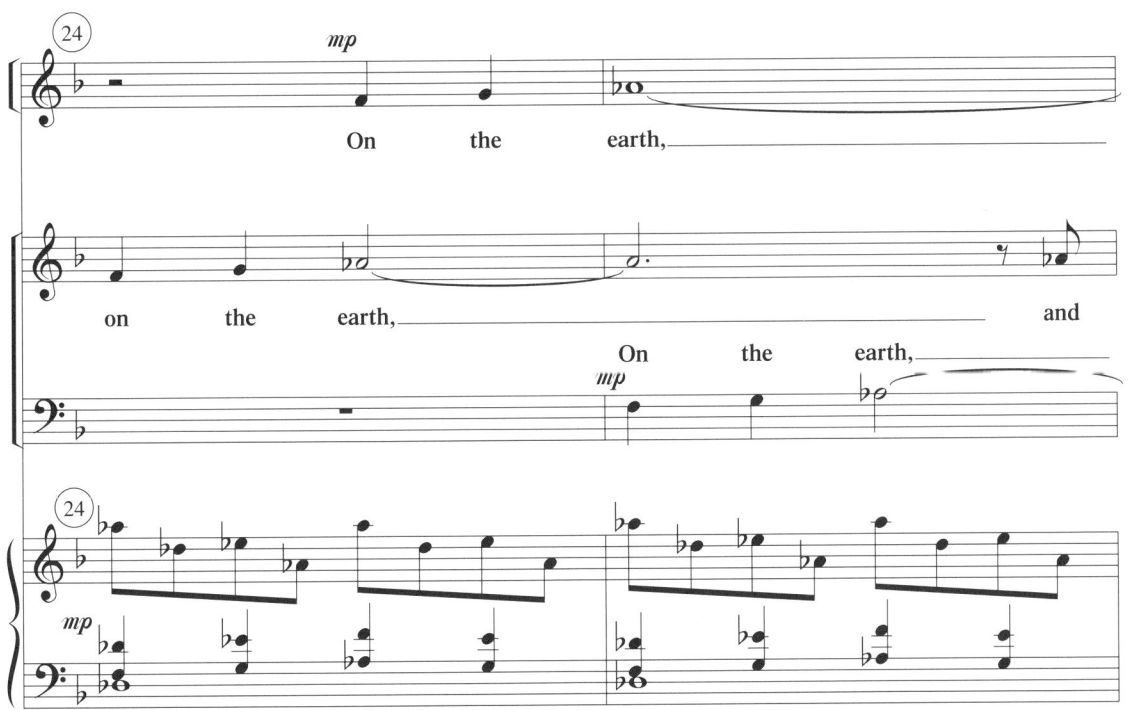

poco a poco cresc.
on the earth,
poco a poco cresc.
on the earth, and
on the earth,
poco a poco cresc.
poco a poco cresc.
28
on the earth
Divisi
on the earth
on the earth
Divisi
28

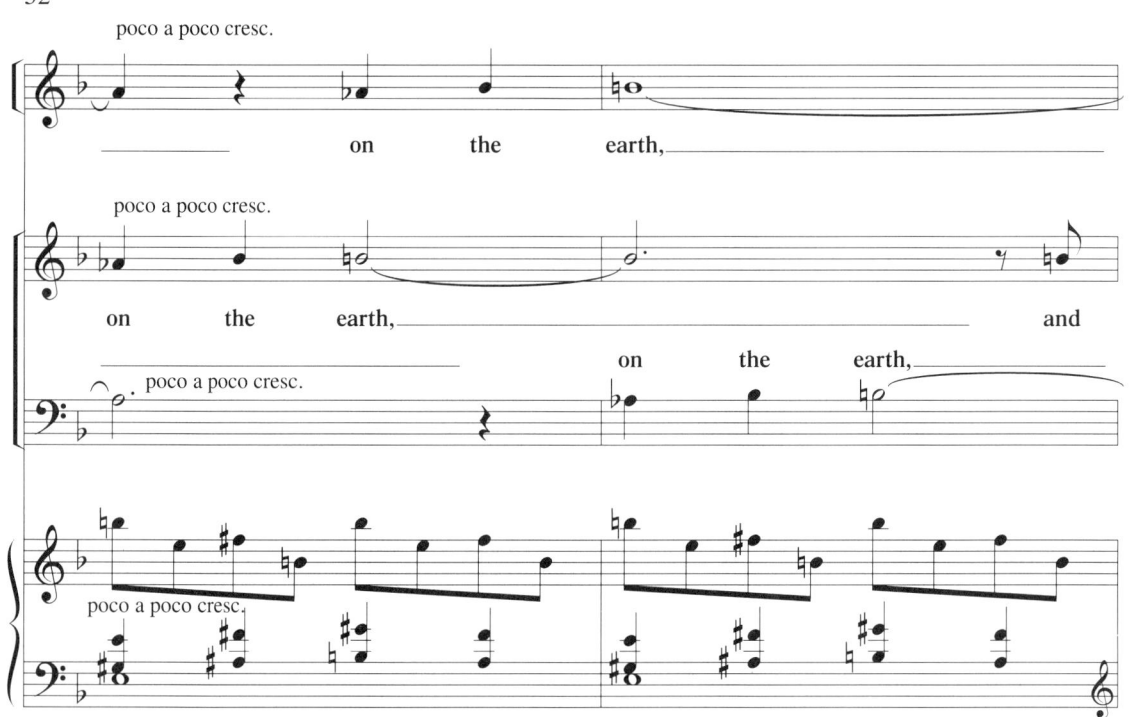

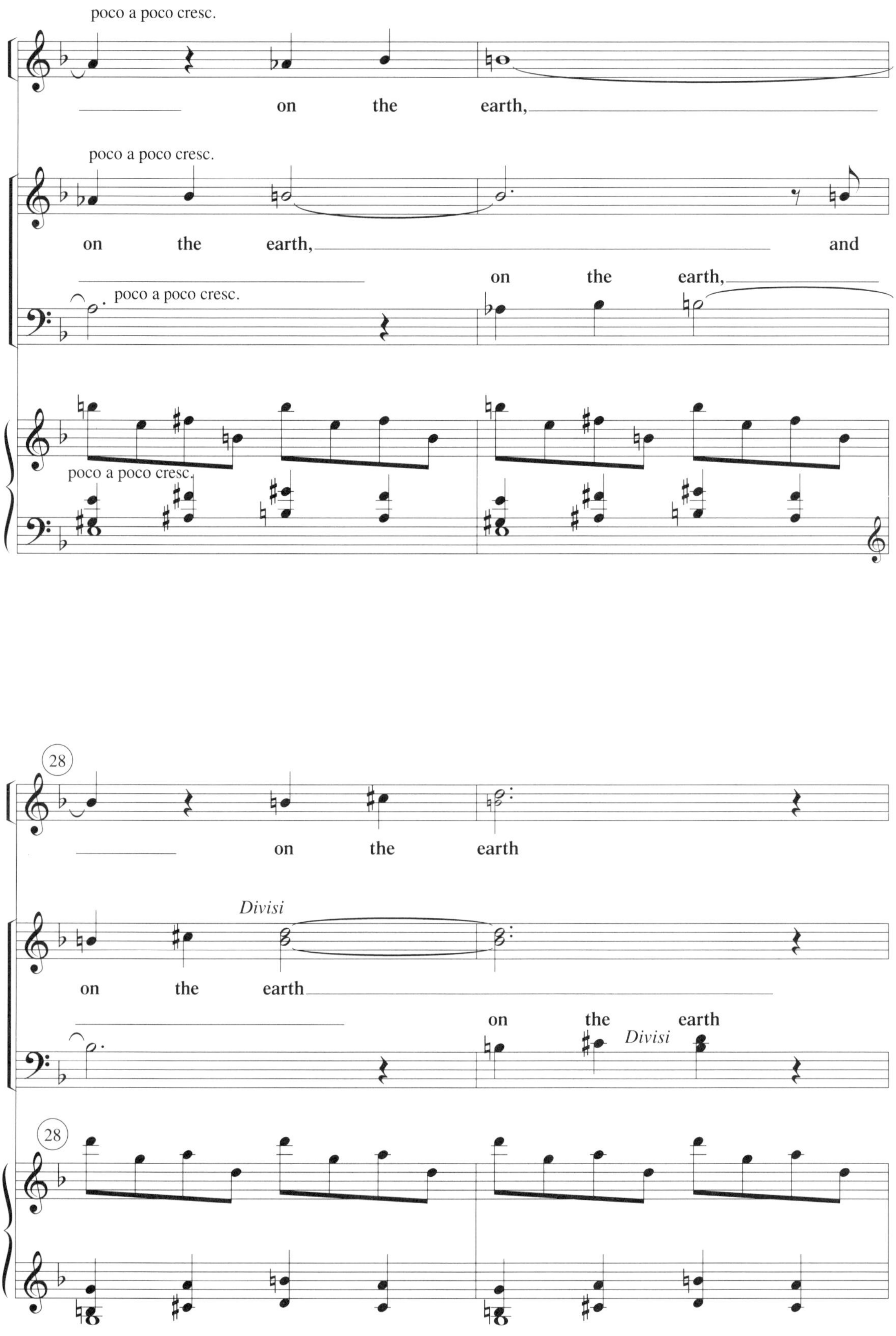

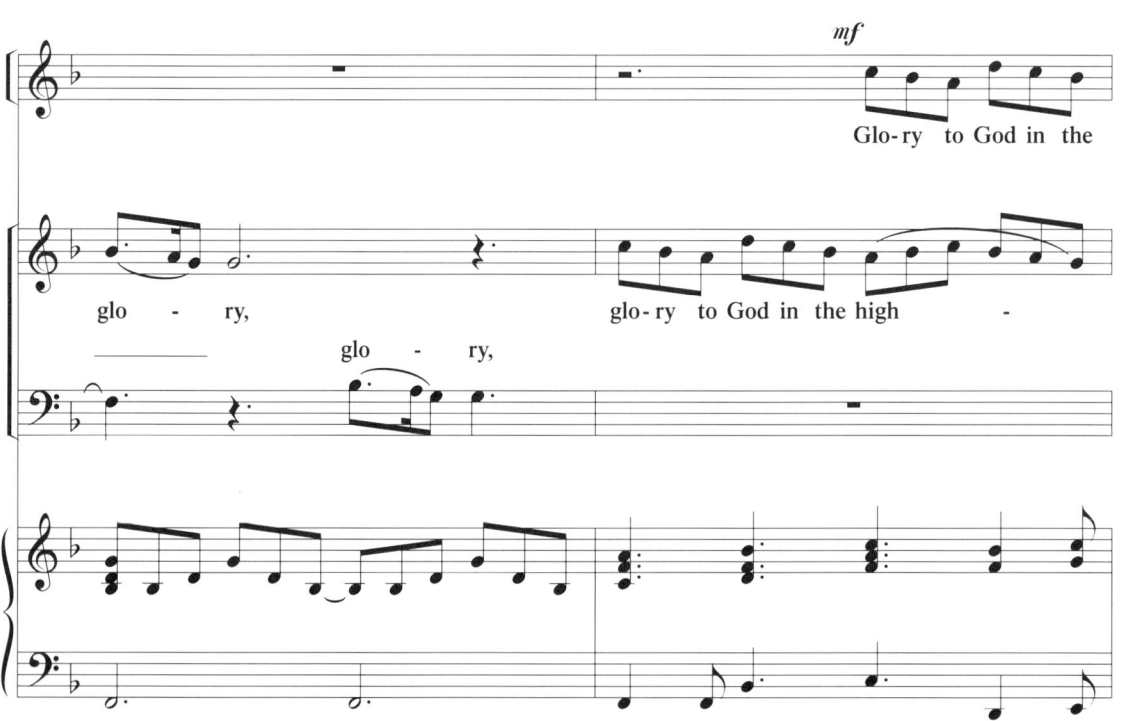

Part VI
JESUS, SHEPHERDS AND CHILDREN
includes
While Shepherds Watched Their Flocks
Christmas Is a Time for Children
Hark, the Herald Angels Sing
Angels, from the Realms of Glory
Go, Tell It on the Mountain

Arranged by Tom Fettke

*"While Shepherds Watched Their Flocks"

**CHILD 1: What can I give Him, poor as I am?
If I were a shepherd, I would give Him a lamb.
CHILD 2: If I were a wise man, I would do my part.
But what can I give Him? *(pause)*
BOTH CHILDREN: I can give Him my heart.

*Music by George Frederick Handel. Arr. © 1998 by Pilot Point Music (ASCAP). All rights reserved. Administered by The Copyright Company, 40 Music Square East, Nashville, TN 37203.

*"Christmas Is a Time for Children"
Children's choir

*Words and Music by Otis Skillings. © 1984 Bud John Songs (ASCAP). All Rights Administered by EMI Christian Music Publishing. All Rights Reserved. Used by Permission.

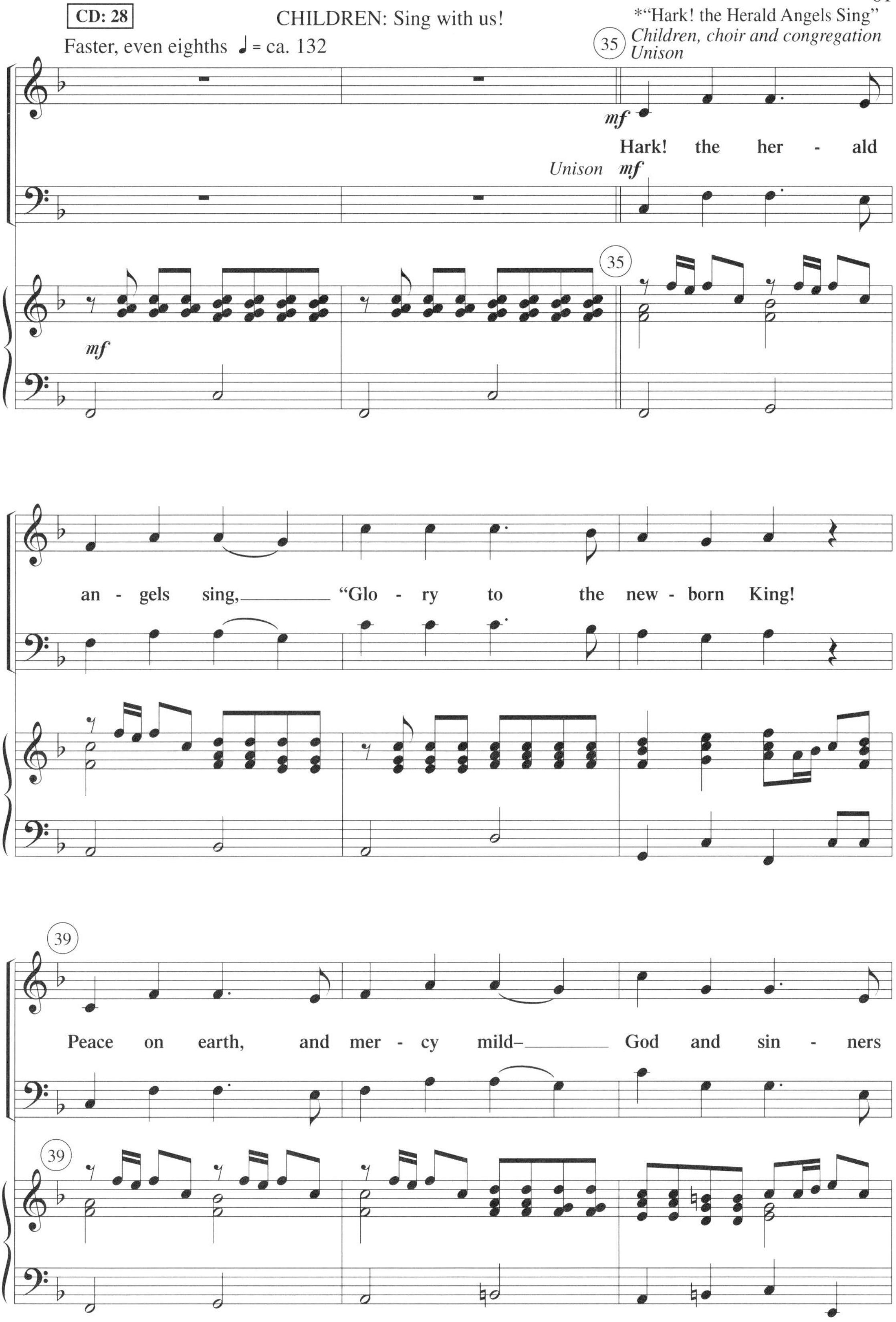

*Words by Charles Wesley; Music by Felix Mendelssohnn. Arr. Admin. by The Copyright Company, 40 Music Square East, Nashville TN 37203.

*Words by James Montgomery; Music by Henry T. Smart. Arr. © 1998 by Pilot Point Music (ASCAP). All rights reserved. Admin. by The Copyright Company, 40 Music Square East, Nashville TN 37203.

65

*Words by John W. Work, Jr.; Music, Afro-American Spiritual. Arr. © 1998 by Pilot Point Music (ASCAP). All rights reserved. Administered by The Copyright Company, 40 Music Square East, Nashville TN 37203.

94
Children
cresc.
For chil - dren like you and
Choir
cresc.
For chil - dren like you and
cresc.
94
cresc.
ff
me.
ff
me.
ff
Straight eighths
8va

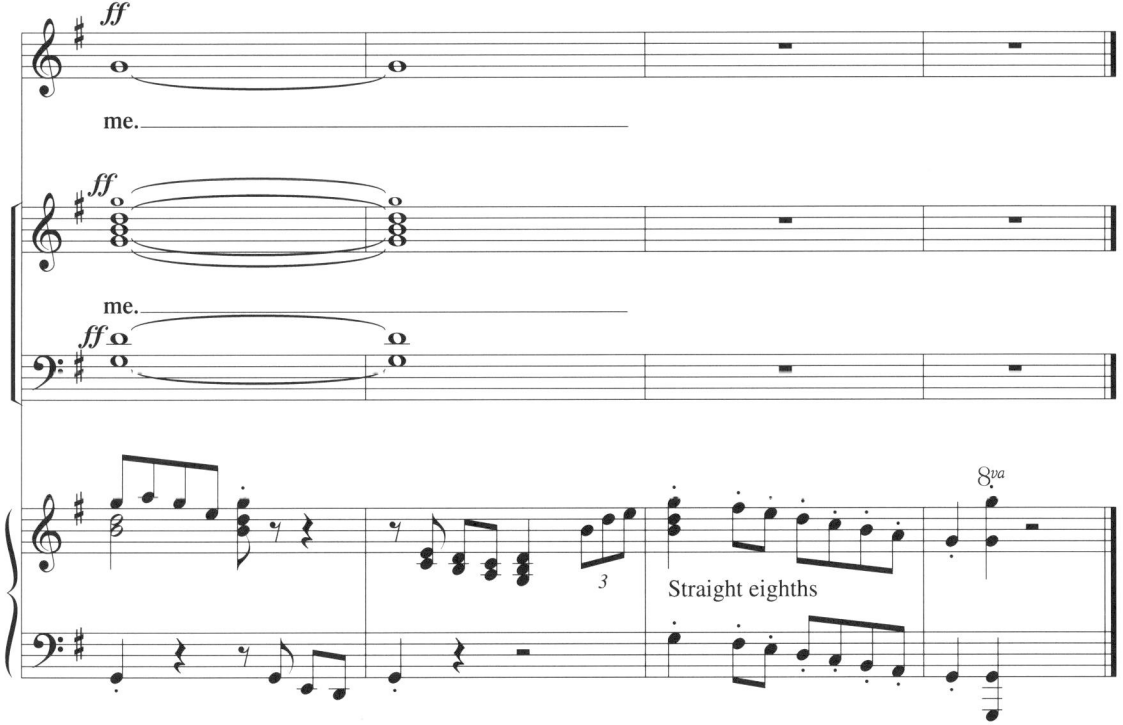

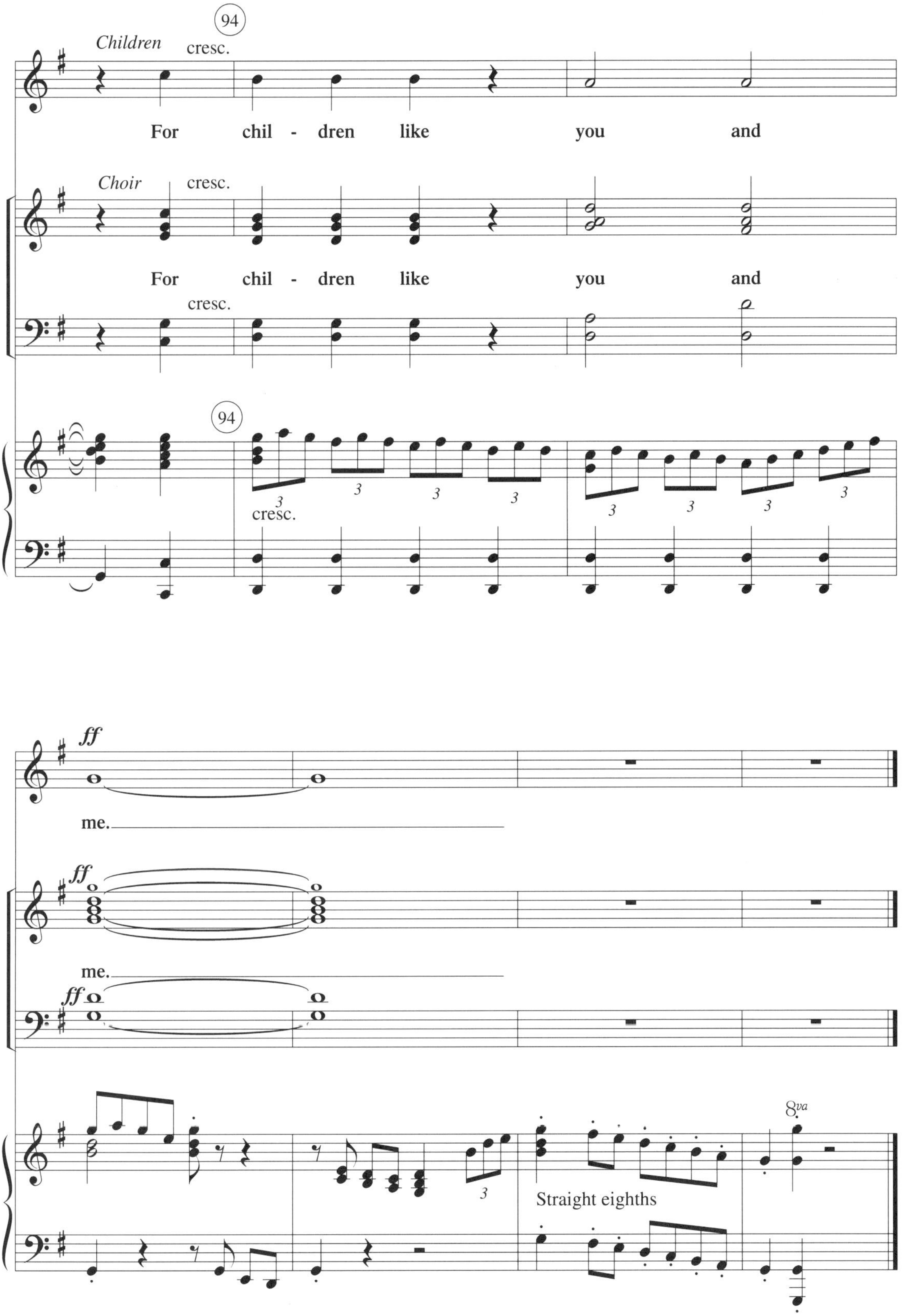

Part VII

REJOICE WITH EXCEEDING GREAT JOY

includes
Nations Will Come to Your Light
Concerto in G Minor
Rejoice with Exceeding Great Joy

*Arranged by Tom Fettke
and Bill Wolaver*

*Words adapted from Isaiah 60:3 by Tom Fettke; Music by Tom Fettke. Copyright © 1998 by Pilot Point Music (ASCAP). All rights reserved. Admin. by The Copyright Company, 40 Music Square East, Nashville, TN 37203.

**Music by Antonio Vivaldi. Arr. © 1998 by Pilot Point Music (ASCAP). All rights reserved. Admin. by The Copyright Company, 40 Music Square E., Nashville, TN 37203.

*Words by Robin Wolaver; Music by Bill Wolaver. Copyright © 1998 by Pilot Point Music (ASCAP). All rights reserved. Admin. by The Copyright Company, 40 Music Square East, Nashville TN 37203.

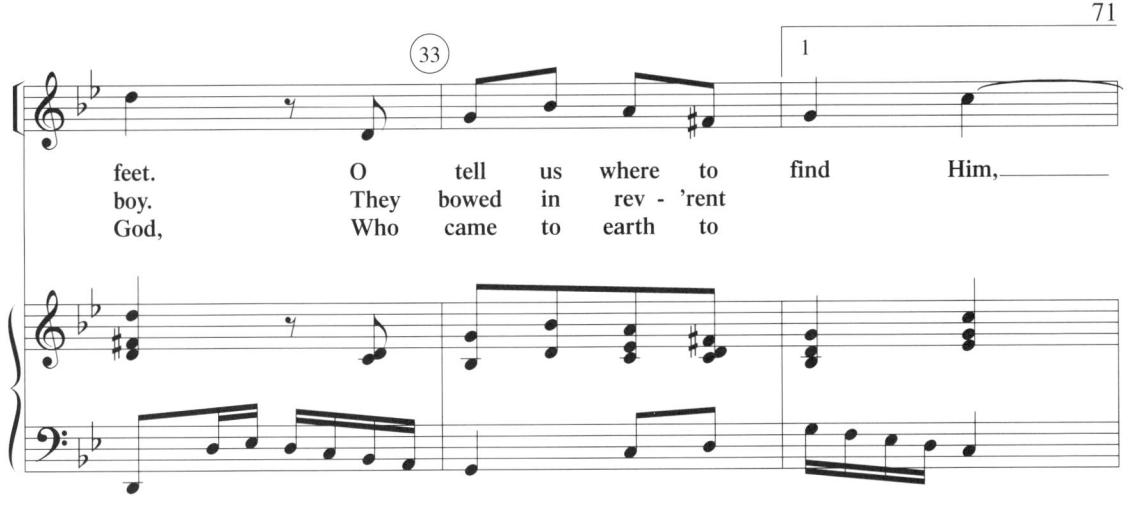

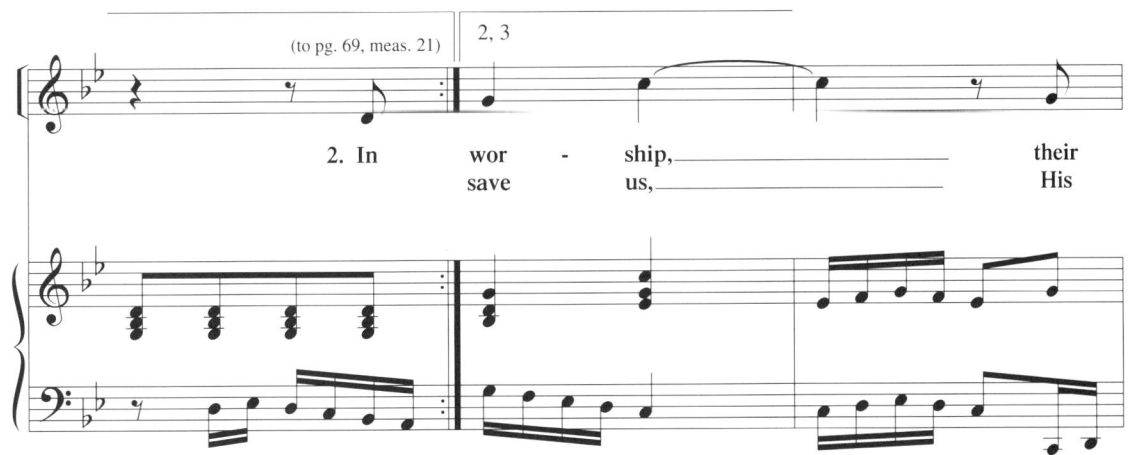

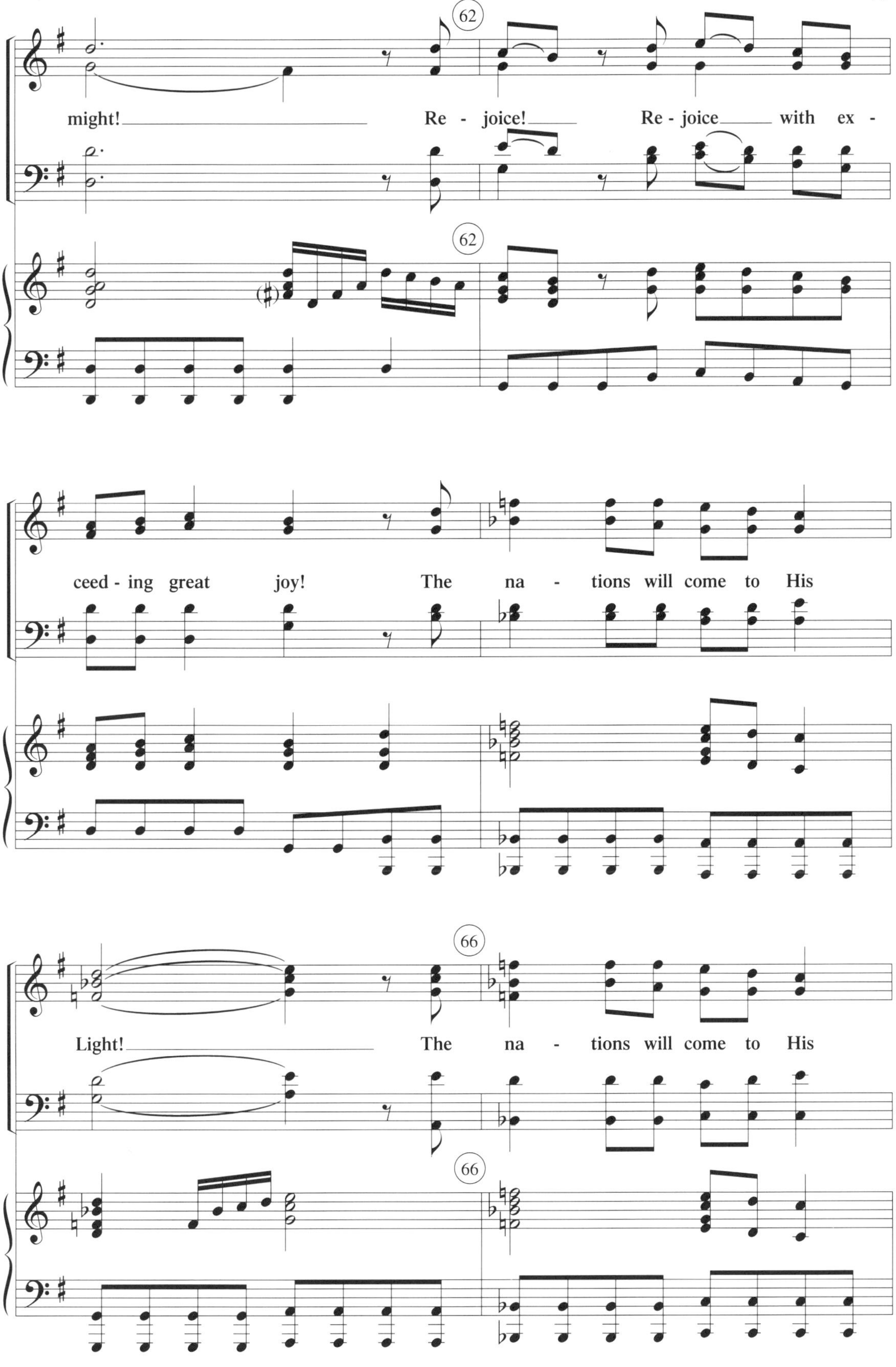
62
might! Re - joice! Re - joice with ex -
62
ceed - ing great joy! The na - tions will come to His
66
Light! The na - tions will come to His
66

Part VIII
GLORY TO THE LAMB OF CHRISTMAS

includes
The Lamb of Christmas
The Lamb Appears

Arranged by Tom Fettke

*"The Lamb of Christmas"
**Acappella preferred

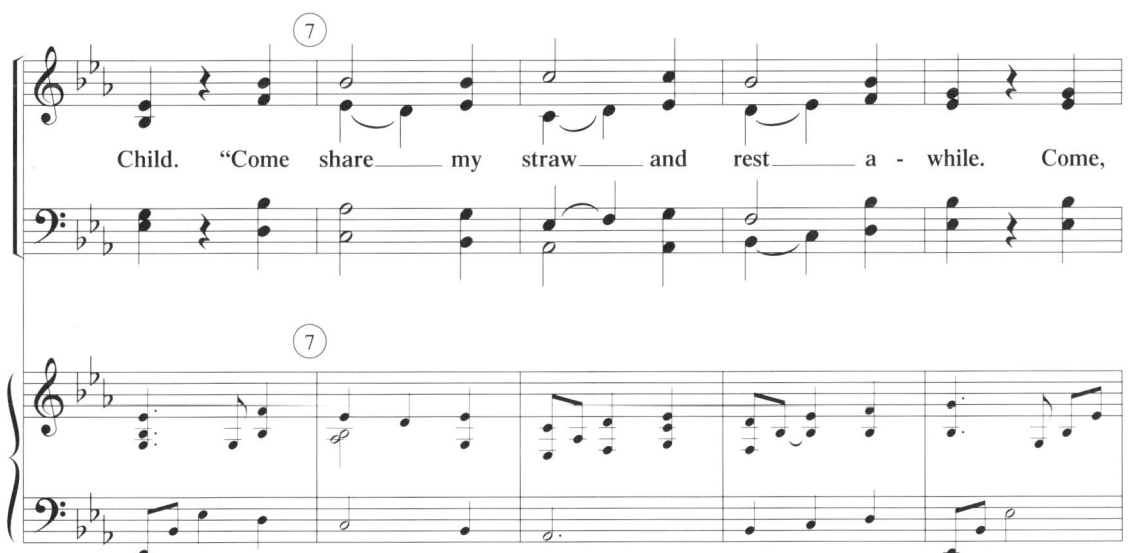

*Words by Ken Bible; Music, Traditional English Melody (*The Friendly Beasts*). Copyright © 1998 by Pilot Point Music (ASCAP). All rights reserved Administered by The Copyright Company, 40 Music Square East, Nashville TN 37203.

**No accompaniment is provided on the accompaniment trax. If support is needed, a live keyboard may be used.

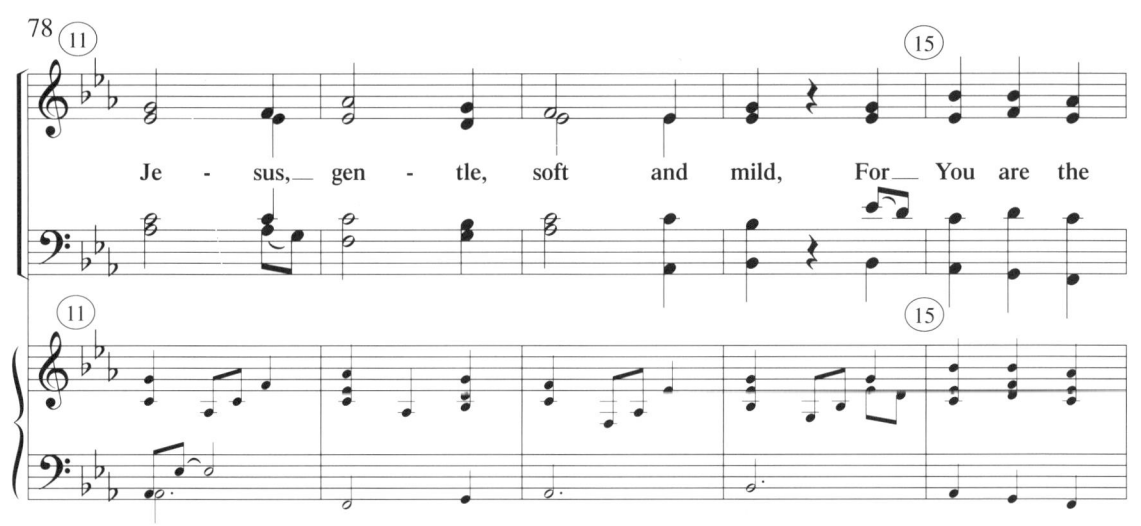
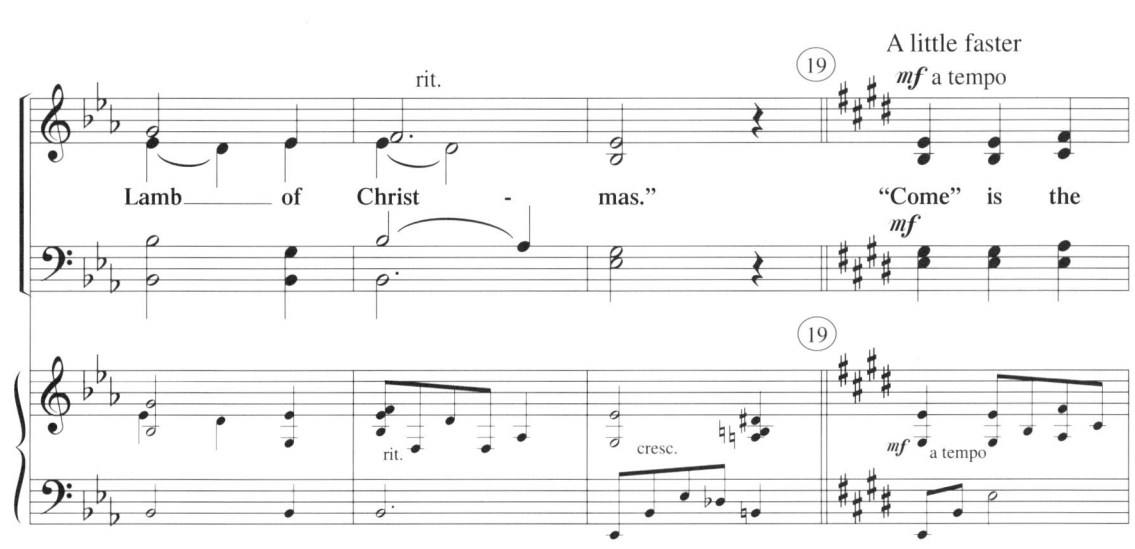
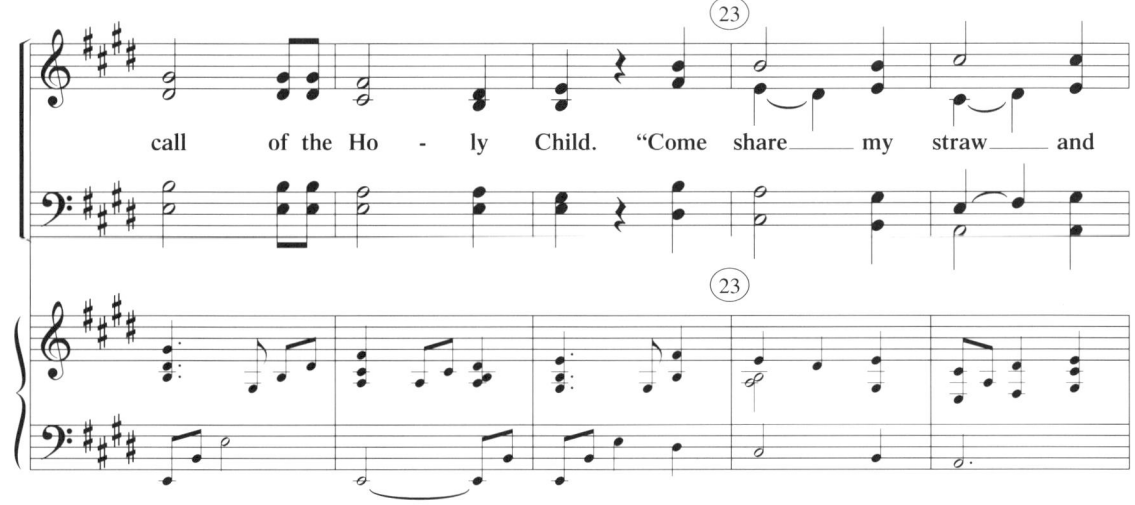

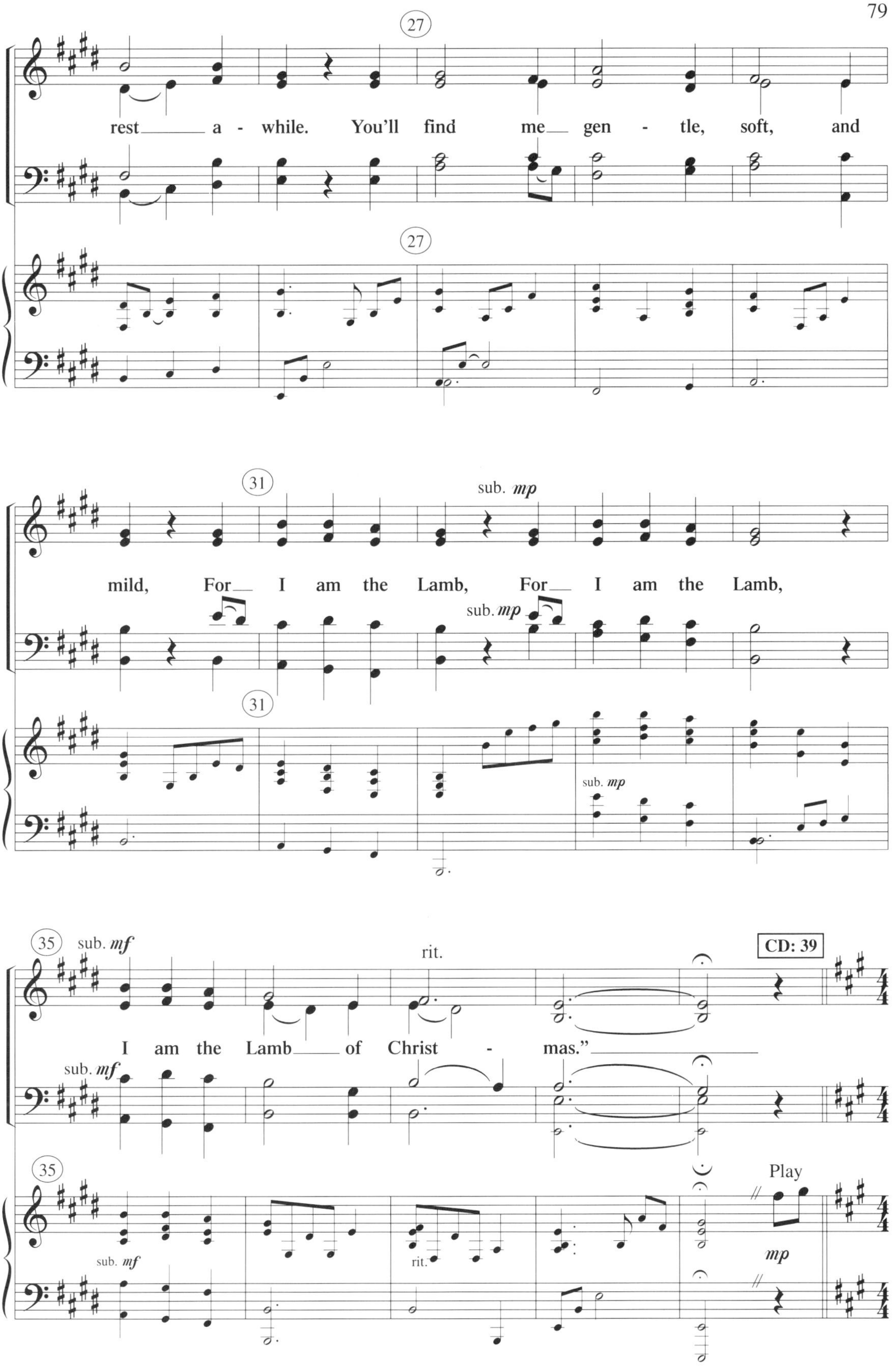
27
rest a - while. You'll find me gen - tle, soft, and
27
31
sub. mp
mild, For I am the Lamb, For I am the Lamb,
sub. mp
31
sub. mp
35
sub. mf
rit.
CD: 39
I am the Lamb of Christ - mas."
sub. mf
35
sub. mf
rit.
Play
mp

*Words adapted from Edward Caswall, with original lyrics by Dennis and Deborah Criser; Music by Dennis and Deborah Criser. Copyright © 1998 by Lillenas Publishing Company (SESAC). All rights reserved. Administered by The Copyright Company, 40 Music Square East, Nashville TN 37203.

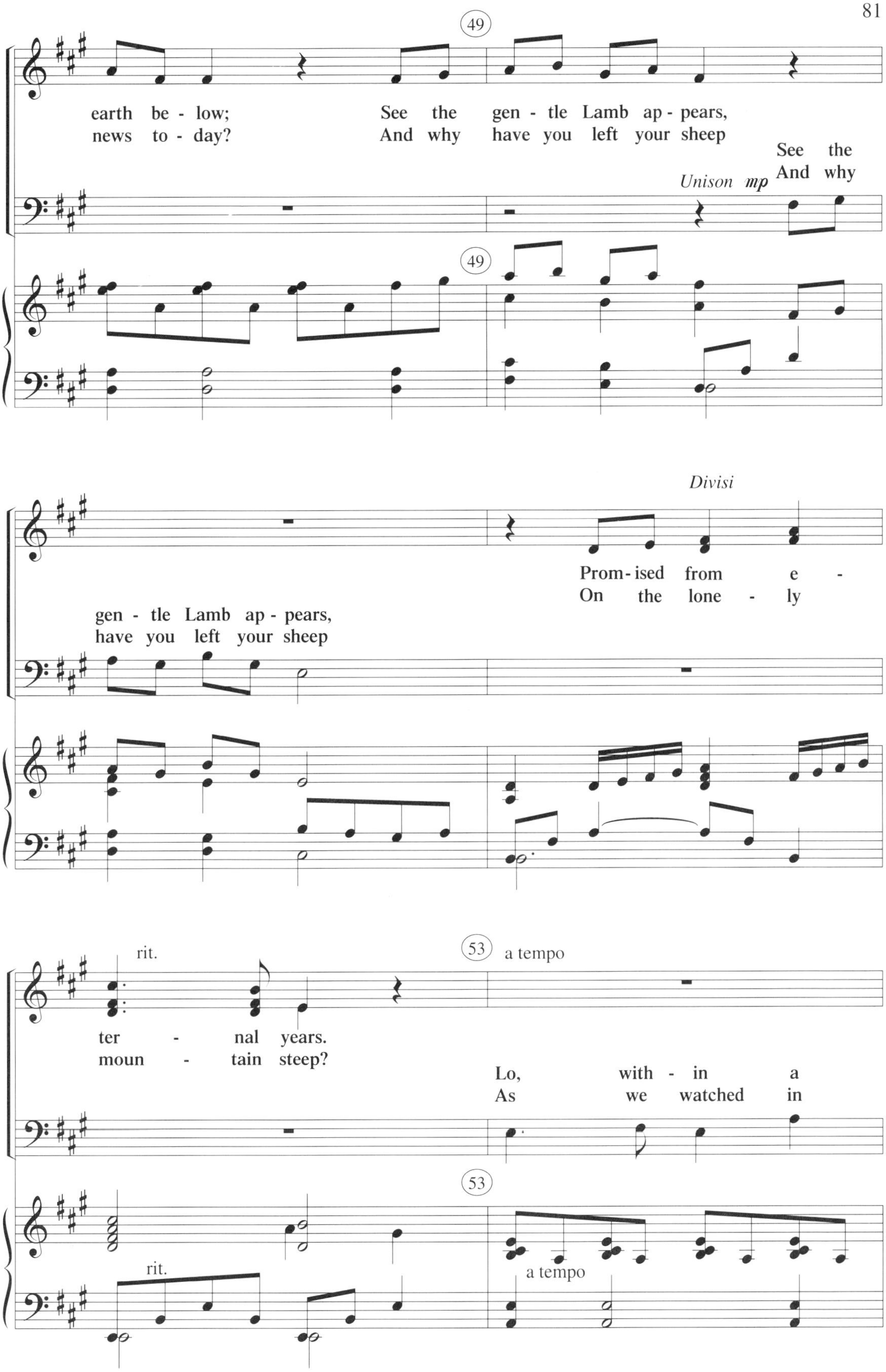
49
earth be - low; See the gen - tle Lamb ap - pears,
news to - day? And why have you left your sheep
Unison mp
See the
And why
49
Divisi
Prom - ised from e -
On the lone - ly
gen - tle Lamb ap - pears,
have you left your sheep
rit.
53
a tempo
ter - nal years.
moun - tain steep?
Lo, with - in a
As we watched in
53
rit.
a tempo

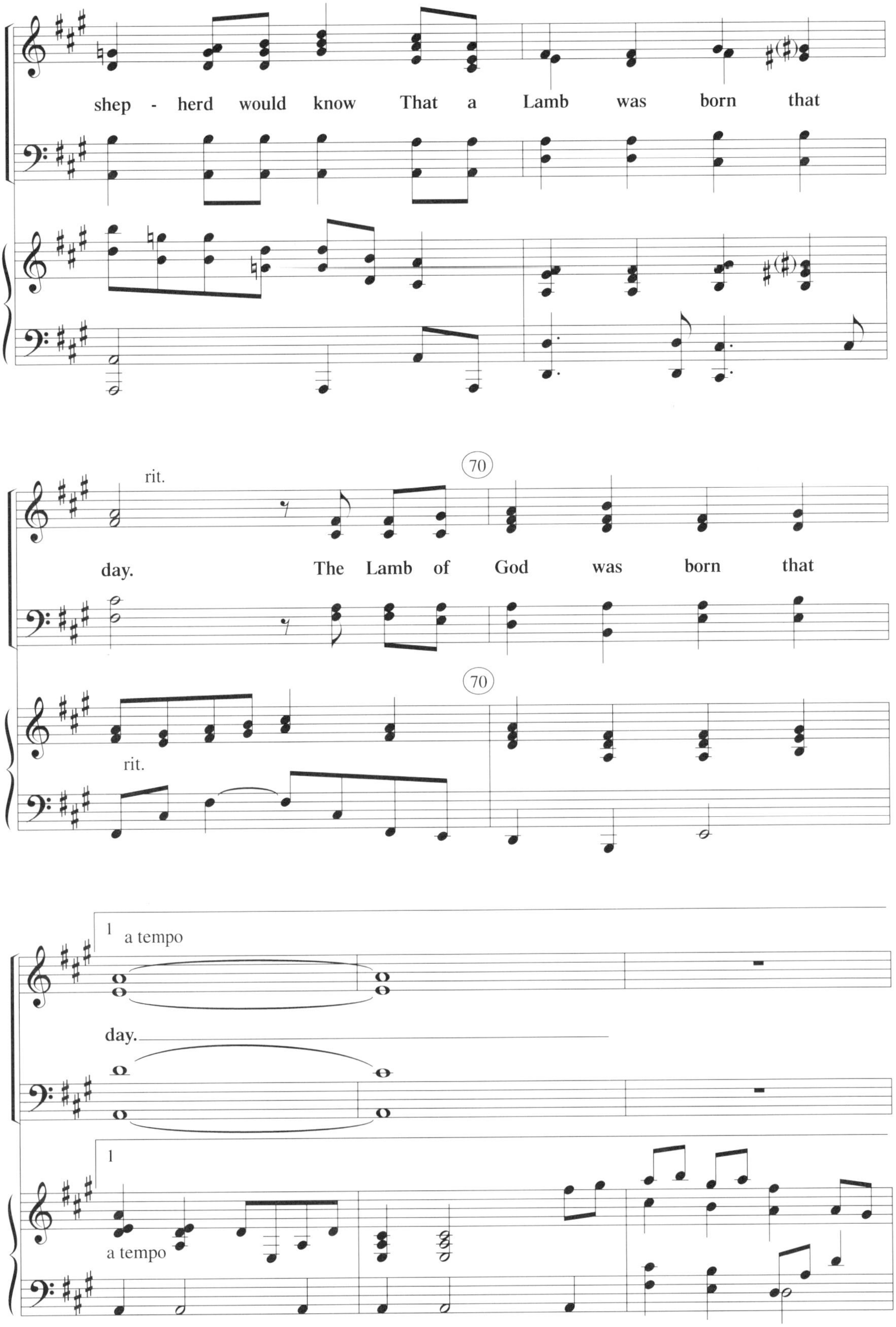
shep - herd would know That a Lamb was born that
rit.
70
day. The Lamb of God was born that
70
rit.
1 a tempo
day.
1
a tempo

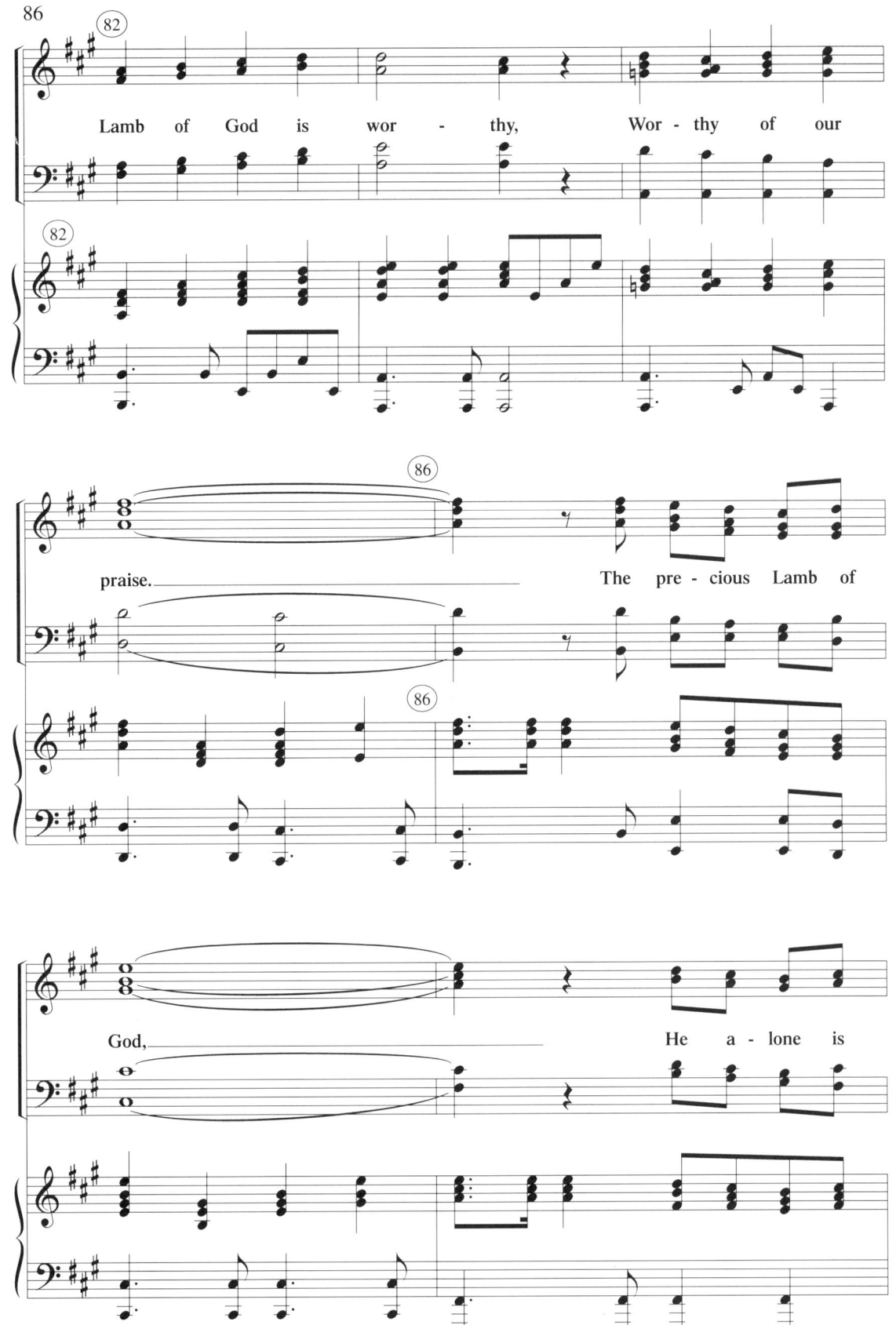

*Words and music by Bill Wolaver and Tom Fettke. Copyright © 1998 by Pilot Point Music (ASCAP). All rights reserved. Admin. by The Copyright Company, 40 Music Square East, Nashville TN 37203.

*"The Glory of the Lord"

*Words by Robin Wolaver; Music by Bill Wolaver. Copyright © 1998 by Pilot Point Music (ASCAP). All rights reserved. Admin. by The Copyright Company, 40 Music Square East, Nashville TN 37203.

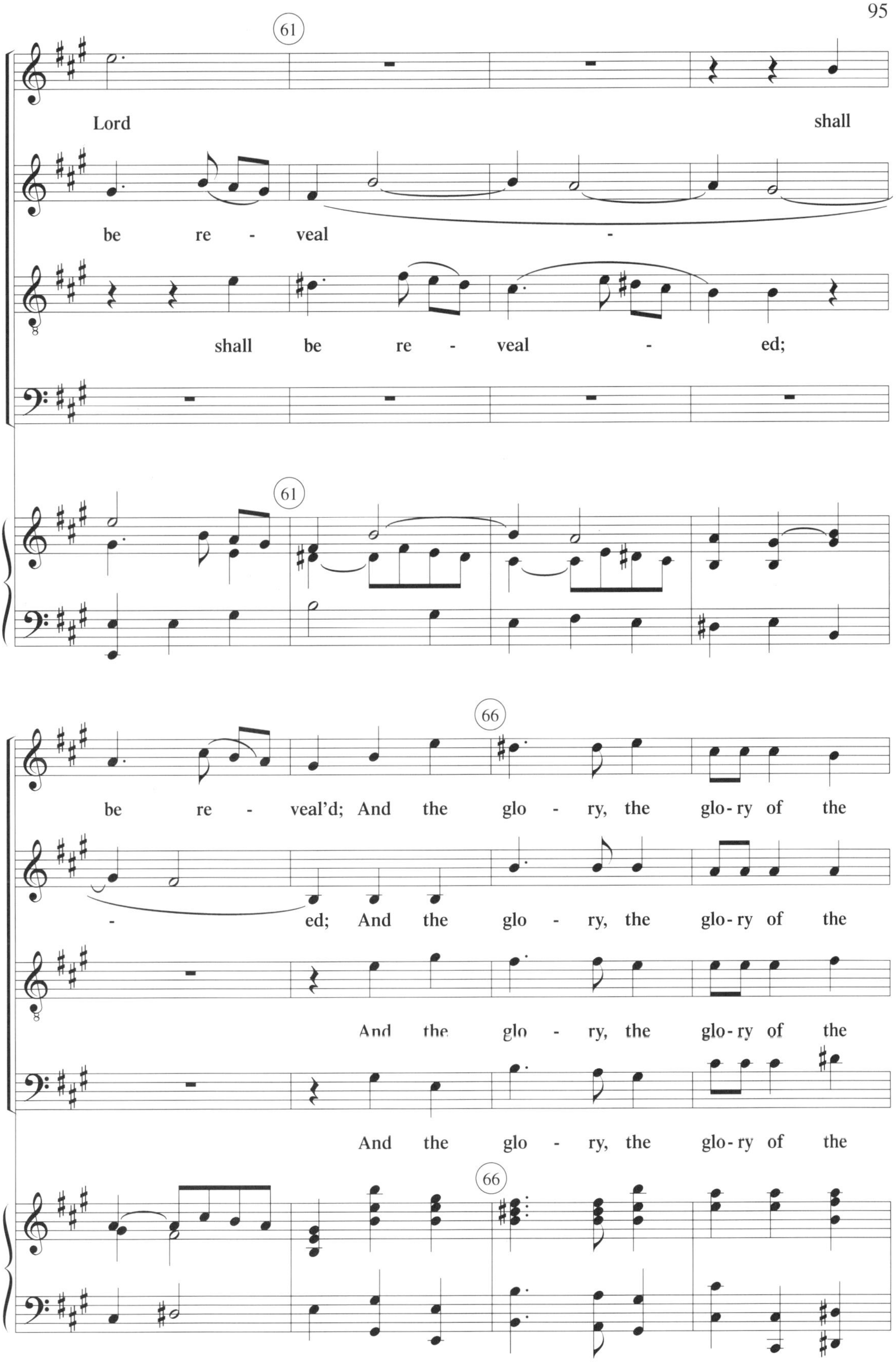
61
Lord shall
be re - veal -
shall be re - veal - ed;
61
be re - veal'd; And the glo - ry, the glo-ry of the
- ed; And the glo - ry, the glo-ry of the
And the glo - ry, the glo-ry of the
And the glo - ry, the glo-ry of the
66
66

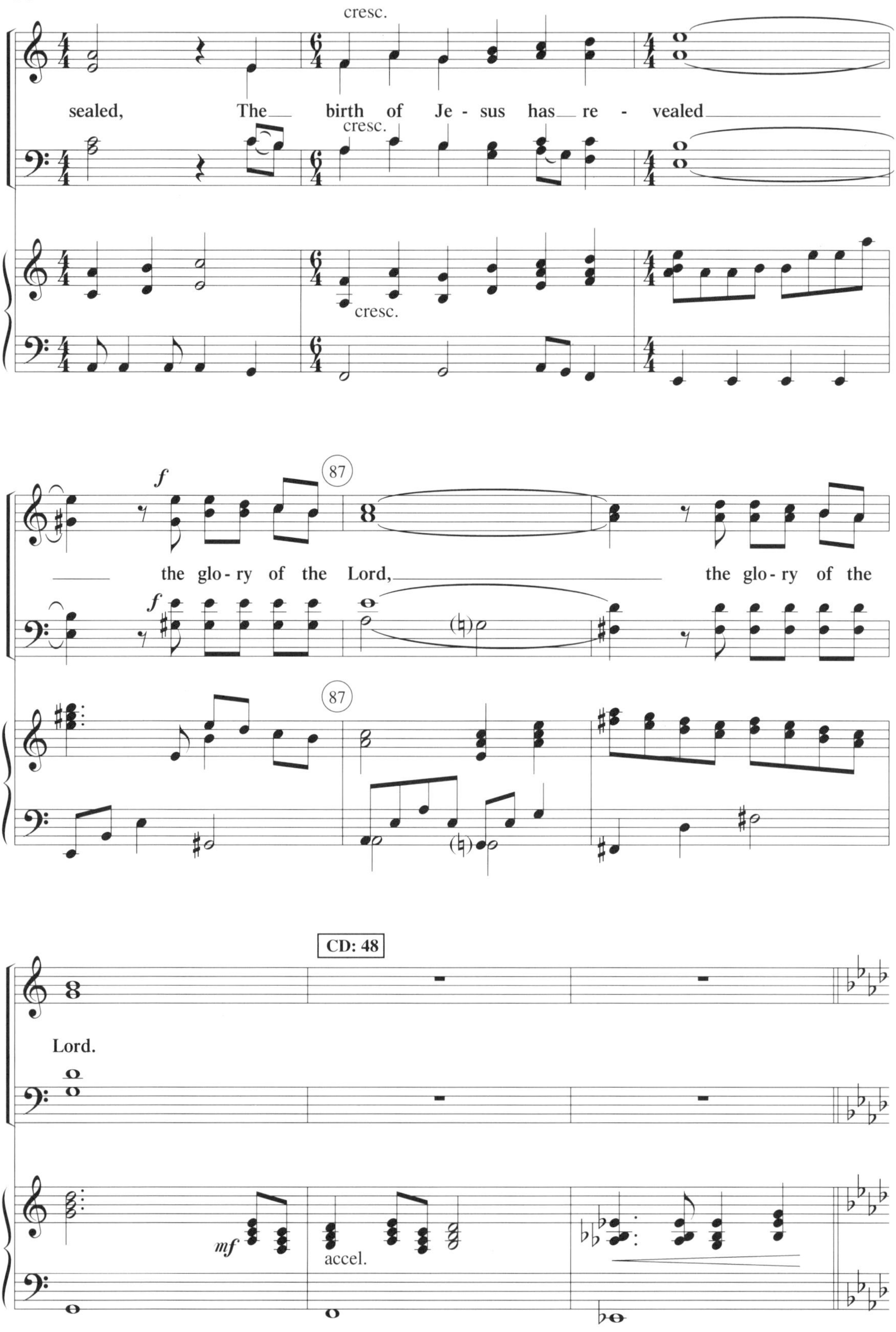
cresc.
sealed, The birth of Je - sus has re - vealed
cresc.
cresc.
f
87
the glo - ry of the Lord, the glo - ry of the
f
87
CD: 48
Lord.
mf
accel.

*"Light Is Shining All Around"

*Words by Ken Bible; Music, Traditional and by Ken Bible. Copyright © 1998 by Pilot Point Music (ASCAP). All rights reserved. Administered by The Copyright Company, 40 Music Square East, Nashville TN 37203.

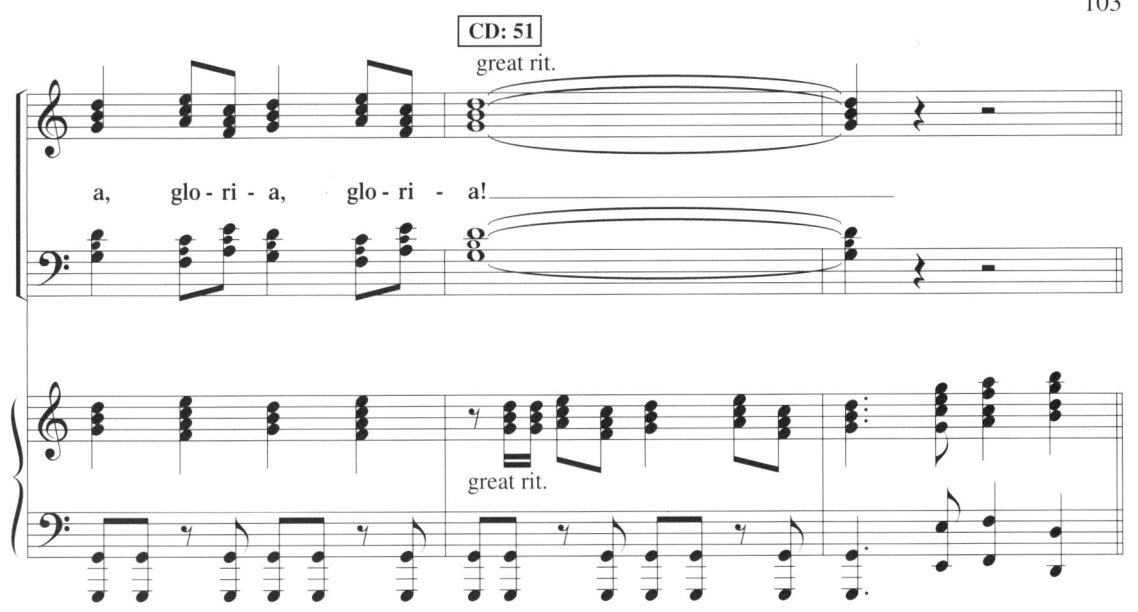

*"Hallelujah Chorus"

*Words adapted from Scripture; Music by George Frederick Handel. Ed. © 1998 by Pilot Point Music (ASCAP). All rights reserved. Administered by The Copyright Company, 40 Music Square East, Nashville TN 37203.

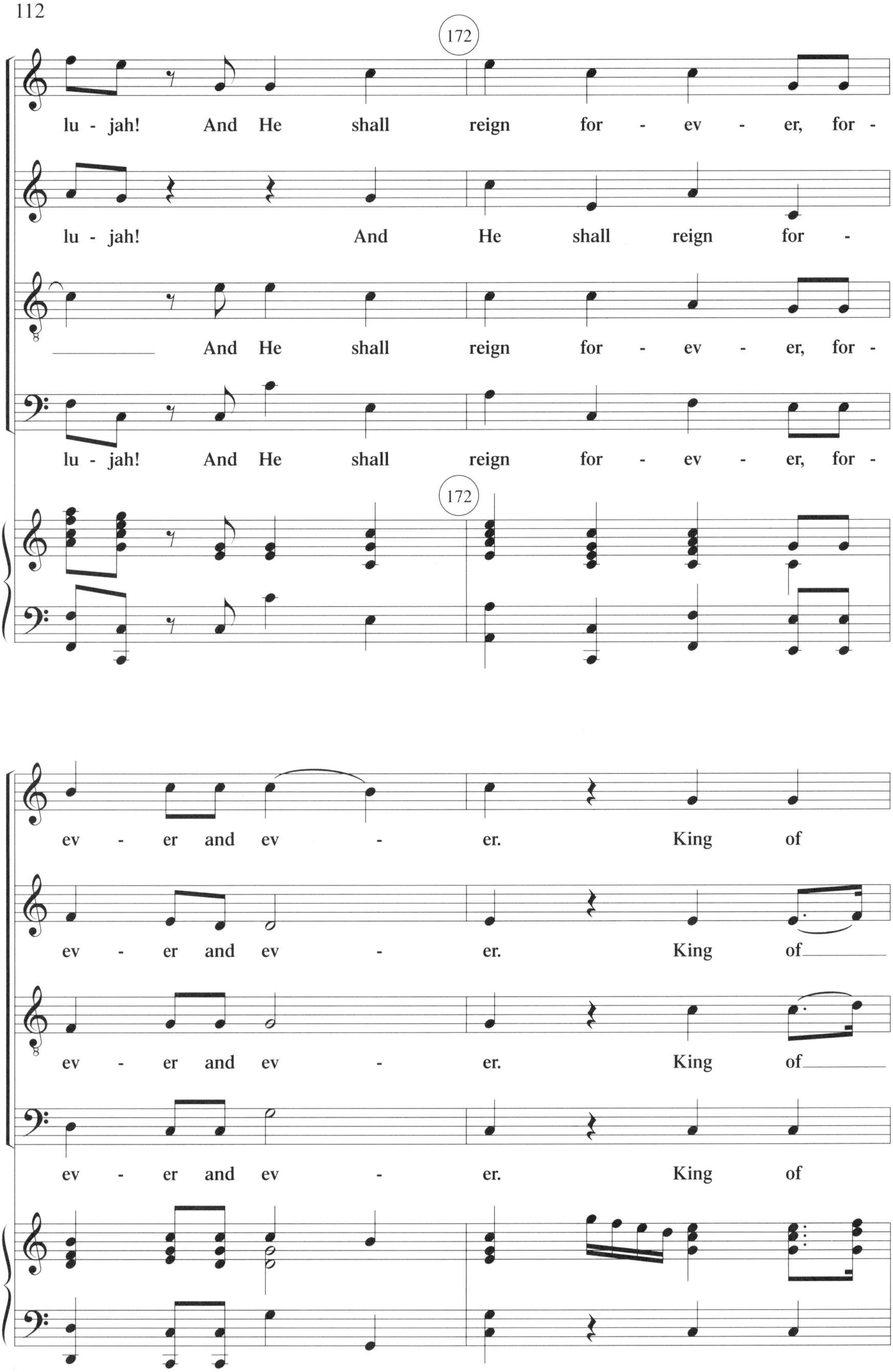
172
lu - jah! And He shall reign for - ev - er, for -
lu - jah! And He shall reign for -
And He shall reign for - ev - er, for -
lu - jah! And He shall reign for - ev - er, for -
172
ev - er and ev - er. King of
ev - er and ev - er. King of
ev - er and ev - er. King of
ev - er and ev - er. King of

175 Kings and Lord of Lords! King of

Kings and Lord of Lords! King of

Kings and Lord of Lords! King of

Kings and Lord of Lords! King of

Kings and Lord of Lords! And

Kings and Lord of Lords! And

Kings and Lord of Lords! And

Kings and Lord of Lords! And He shall

GLORIA
IN
EXCELSIS
DEO

GLORIA
IN
EXCELSIS
DEO

GLORIA
IN
EXCELSIS
DEO

GLORIA
IN
EXCELSIS
DEO

GLORIA
IN
EXCELSIS
DEO

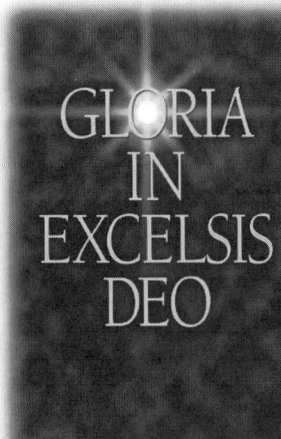